UP AGAINST IT

Up Against it was originally commissioned for the Beatles as the film to follow *Help*. But they reckoned without Joe Orton's predilection for outrageous black farce. 'The boys, in my script,' he wrote, 'have been caught in-flagrante, become involved in dubious political activity, dressed as women, committed murder, been put in prison and committed adultery.'

The Beatles never made the film, but the screenplay survives, alongside *Loot, What the Butler Saw, Entertaining Mr Sloane* and Orton's other plays, as yet another testament to his extraordinary talent.

The story behind the writing of *Up Against It* — Orton's bizarre encounters with the Beatles' entourage, and his death on the very morning he was due to discuss the filming — is recounted in the introduction by John Lahr, author of Orton's biography, Prick Up Your Ears.

by the same author

Entertaining Mr Sloane
Loot
Crimes of Passion
What the Butler Saw
Funeral Games and The Good and Faithful Servant

The Complete Plays

Joe Orton

Up against it

A SCREENPLAY FOR THE BEATLES

Introduced by John Lahr

EYRE METHUEN · LONDON

First published in 1979 by Eyre Methuen Ltd
11 New Fetter Lane, London EC4P 4EE
Copyright © 1979 by the Estate of Joe Orton, deceased
Introduction Copyright © 1979 by John Lahr
Extracts from the private diaries of Joe Orton
Copyright © 1979 by the Estate of Joe Orton, deceased
Set IBM Journal by 𝒜 Tek-Art, Croydon, Surrey
Printed in Great Britain by Fakenham Press Ltd, Fakenham,
Norfolk

ISBN 0 413 45980 2

Introduction

'Well, the sound and the fury is over', Orton wrote to an American friend in October 1966. 'LOOT and JOE ORTON (as you can see from the reviews) a great success. I feel exhausted. 18 months of struggling to vindicate the honour of my play (my own is beyond vindication) have left me weak at the knees.'

By January 1967, Orton's sense of exhaustion had given way to exhilaration. He had just turned 34. His reputation had been secured. The grind of *Loot's* rewrites had paid off not only in acclaim but in craft. And Orton knew it. He was riding high and entering the most fecund period of his literary life. His career had acquired a new velocity. By the second week of January, the first draft of his farce masterpiece *What the Butler Saw* was completed and tucked away in the drawer beneath his divan bed to 'mature' for six months. A TV production of *The Good and Faithful Servant* with Donald Pleasance was in rehearsal. *Entertaining Mr Sloane*, after being scuttled by ITV, was rescheduled. *Loot* had been bought for Broadway. And on January 11, Orton stepped up to the podium at Quaglino's in a large flowered tie and a wide grin to accept the *Evening Standard* Award for the Best Play of the Year.

'I was on the front of the Evening Standard receiving the award,' Orton wrote in the diary he'd begun a few weeks earlier and puckishly called *Diary of a Somebody*, 'I'm very happy.' The word 'happy' is so rare in Orton's diaries as to be startling. He distrusted happiness; and in this case, it didn't last long. The TV programme that broadcast the ceremony ran its credits over Orton receiving the award. 'The whole had the effect of the man with the bladder hitting the Emperor on the head as he rode in triumph. Just to take him down a peg and remind him that he wasn't a god.'

But Orton was in a weird state of grace, and even this minor disappointment was quickly forgotten the next day when Orton was contacted to work on a film script for the Beatles. In the aristocracy of success, Orton was learning fast, there were no strangers.

Orton had never written a film script. In 1964, he worked up a nineteen page treatment for Lindsay Anderson who wanted to make a modern movie version of *The Bacchae*. The film never got off the ground; and Orton turned his notion into *The Erpingham Camp*. Funny as Orton's treatment was, his arch style didn't seem to suit the camera. 'Not film dialogue, is it?' was Lindsay Anderson's verdict. But since then, Orton's understanding of plot and tone had become more sophisticated. In his rewrites of *Loot* and the first draft of *What the Butler Saw* he worked hard to make his stage pictures as startling as his words. His comedy was becoming more visual. To match the Beatles' high jinks with his own wicked fun was an irresistible challenge. Always the tease, Orton tried to hide his enthusiasm when Walter Shenson called him. Shenson, who had produced *A Hard Day's Night* and *Help*, wanted Orton to 'punch-up' a dull script the Beatles had already commissioned. Orton recorded the conversation in his diary:

'Would you like to see it with a view to working on the film script?' I was very impressed by this, but I put on a nonchalant manner. 'Well, I'm frightfully up to my eyes in it at the moment', I said. 'I'm writing my third play'. 'I'd certainly love to have you take a look at this draft', he said. 'I've discussed it with the boys. I mean I mentioned your name to them. They've heard of you. They didn't react too much, I must say. But I think I can persuade them to have you.' By this time I was feeling foolish and not at all nonchalant. 'Yes', I said. 'Please send the script over and I'll read it.'

Orton read the Beatles' script on January 15, the day he re-read the first draft of *What the Butler Saw* ('Pleased, but still work to be done'). After such hard and inspired writing, he needed a change of pace; and the Beatles' script promised to be more a romp than a slog. He was full of fun and ideas. And, besides, the script had possibilities.

Like the idea. Basically it is that there aren't four young men. Just four aspects of one man. Sounds dreary, but as I thought about it I realised what wonderful opportunities it would give. The end in the present script is the girl advancing on the four to accept a proposal of marriage from one of them (which, the script coyly says, we shall never know). Already have the idea that the end should be a church with four bridegrooms and one bride. THE HOMECOMING in fact, but alibied in such a way that no one could object. Lots of opportunities for sexual ambiguities — a woman's bedroom at night, her husband out-side and four men inside. I also would like to incorporate a lot of material from the first novel Kenneth [Halliwell] and I wrote called THE SILVER BUCKET. In it a young girl is expelled from her native village for some unnamed offence. Already see how it could be one boy expelled from some great industrial metropolis by a ceremony of mammoth proportions. Could be funny. As long as I wasn't expected to write a naturalistic script. Rang Walter Shenson . . . Arranged to meet him tomorrow.

Basically the Beatles are getting fed up with the Dick Lester type of direction. They want dialogue to speak. Also they are tired of actors like Leon McKern [sic] stealing scenes. Difficult this as I don't think any of the Beatles can act in any accepted sense. As Marilyn Monroe couldn't act. Hope to discuss this problem in detail tomorrow.

Before seeing Shenson, Orton met with his agent Peggy Ramsay. It was nearly three years to the week since she'd summoned him to her office in St Martin's Lane and agreed to represent *Entertaining Mr Sloane*. As Orton was getting up to leave from that first meeting, she'd asked him what he lived on while he wrote. Orton explained that he was on the dole and surviving on £3.10s. a week. She immediately marshalled her forces and found him a producer within three weeks. Orton's advance on the play had been £100. Now Peggy Ramsay was telling him, 'We'll ask ten thousand. Not a hope of getting it, of course. But we'll allow ourselves to be beaten down.'

'The class of my characters has gone up over the years', Orton observed in 1967. Success had widened his social horizons. Unaccustomed to power and a stranger to abundance, Orton eyed movie moguls like Shenson with a combination of wonder and suspicion. Since 1953, he'd lived a hermetic existence with Kenneth Halliwell in a succession of North London bedsitters. They'd met when both were students at RADA. Halliwell was twenty-four; and Orton was eighteen. Halliwell, who was well-educated, presented himself as a sophisticate; and Orton, then only a provincial lad from Leicester who hadn't even passed his Eleven-plus, saw in him a mentor and a friend. They abandoned acting as a bad bet. and set out to make their fame and fortune in literature. Writing had been Halliwell's idea. He educated Orton to be his constant companion and intellectual equal. They studied and often wrote together. They were inseparable; and only with Orton's success in 1964, did he begin to move outside Halliwell's orbit. 'I'm from the gutter and don't you forget it,' Orton told the producer Oscar Lewenstein, because I won't.' Orton was an outsider; and it was precisely his rejection of the bourgeois world which made his laughter dangerous. Nonetheless, he relished infiltrating alien territory. Any association with the Beatles would put him at the hot centre of pop culture. In meeting Shenson, Orton was taking his first steps down the corridors of commercial power. His diary shows how carefully he watched every move.

I went into a door with a sheet of paper pinned onto it saying 'With the compliments of Walter Shenson (films) Inc.' Inside was a small office. Empty. I looked into a further office. In it was a man about thirty-five, pinkish face, rather a bright, cringing air. 'Are you for Walter?' he said. 'Yes,' I said. 'My name is Joe Orton'. I said this in a bold, confident tone. He squeezed past me in the doorway. 'Walter!' he gave a quick, sharp call. A man appeared in a far doorway. Middle-aged. Short hair going to grey. A bald patch. He started towards me, his hand outstretched. In fact he'd begun the motion of shaking hands before his hand touched mine. 'Come into my office', he said. 'That's the wrong door'. 'I thought it was a bit crummy,' I said. 'For a film producer.' 'Heh, heh, heh,' laughed Walter Shenson. 'Throw your coat over here, heh, heh, heh.' I put down my coat and he disappeared into another office. . . While he was gone I looked around. It was a big, long room. On the shelf over the fireplace was a cube with the faces of the four Beatles on each side of the cube. I picked it up and opened the lid, inside was a card saying 'Horse shit'. 'Heh, heh, heh,' said Walter Shenson, appearing behind me, 'That's a joke thing some guy sent me from back home. They're quite a thing over there, now, heh, heh, heh.'

We talked for a while about the script. I gave away a few of my ideas. Enough to whet his appetite . . . Over lunch he said that one of the ideas for a new Beatles' film was *The Three Musketeers*. 'Oh, no!' I said. 'That's been done to death.' 'Brigitte Bardot wanted to paly Lady de-Winter,' he said. 'She's been done to death as well,' I said. 'Oh, heh, heh, heh, boy!' he said. 'You certainly are quick' . . .

By the end of the day, Orton had a title for his original film script: *Up Against It*, and had written the first two pages. 'Miss Drumgoole and Father Brodie have come to life as interesting characters. Which should delight the Beatles,' he wrote. 'I'm not bothering to write characters for them. I shall just do all my box of tricks — Sloane and Hal on them. After all if I repeat myself in this film it doesn't matter. Nobody who sees the film will have seen *Sloane* or *Loot*.'

The film was a lark, and Orton never invested it with the care or passion he gave his plays. His instructions to Peggy Ramsay on January 25, reflected his insouciance:

'We should ask £15,000', I said, 'and then if they beat us down, remember no lower than 10,000. After all, whether I do it or not is a matter of indifference to me.' Peggy agreed. 'If they won't pay us 10 they can fuck themselves,' I said. 'Of course, darling', Peggy said.

Shenson had promised to arrange a meeting between Orton and the Beatles. In his talk Orton heard the first seductive stroke of the movie rubdown, the slap and tickle of famous names and big paydays:

'You'll be hearing either from Brian Epstein or Paul McCartney [Shenson told Orton on January 17]. So don't be surprised if a Beatle rings you up.' 'What an experience', I said. 'I shall feel as nervous as I would if St Michael, or God was on the line.' 'Oh, there's not any need to be worried, Joe', Shenson said. 'I can say, from my heart that the boys are very respectful of talent. I mean, most respectful of anyone they feel has talent. I can really say that, Joe.'

The Call finally came at dinner time a week later on January 23. 'Epstein's adviser rang while I was eating a meal of mashed potatoes, tinned salmon and beetroot', Orton noted wryly.

Orton arrived promptly the next day at Epstein's office to be faced with the screenwriter's first debilitating hazard: waiting. 'After about five minutes or so a youngish man with a hair-style which was way out in 1958, short, college-boy came up and said, "... I'm Brian Epstein's personal assistant" ' Orton wrote in his diary on January 24.

It crossed my mind to wonder why the English have never got around to finding a perfectly respectable word for 'boy-friend'. 'I'm afraid there's been a most awful mix-up. And all the boys' appointments have been put back an hour and a half'. I was a bit chilly in my manner after that. 'Do you want me to come back at six?' I said. 'Well, no. Could we make another appointment? 'What guarantee is there that you won't break that?' I said. 'I think you better find yourself a different writer.' This said with indifferent success, though the effect was startling. He

asked me to wait a minute and went away to return with Brian
Epstein himself. Somehow I'd expected something like Michael
Codron. I'd imagined Epstein to be florid, Jewish, dark-haired
and overbearing. Instead I was face to face with a mousey-
haired, slight young man. Washed-out in a way. He had a
suburban accent. I went into his office. 'Could you meet Paul
and me for dinner tonight?' he said. 'We do want to have the
pleasure of talking to you.' 'I've a theatre engagement tonight'
I replied, by now sulky and unhelpful. 'Could I send the car to
fetch you after the show?' I didn't much relish this flim-
flammery, left almost tripping over the carpet and crashing
into the secretary who gave a squeal of surprise as I hurtled
past her. This I never mention when re-telling the story. I
always end on a note of hurt dignity.

Orton's first glimpse of the Beatles' world caught the ludicrous
contradiction in these cultural supermen: playing rebel and living
posh.

Arrived in Belgravia at ten minutes to eight . . . I found Chapel
Street easily. I didn't want to get there too early so I walked
around for a while and came back through a nearby mews.
When I got back to the house it was nearly eight o'clock. I
rang the bell and an old man entered. He seemed surprised to
see me. 'Is this Brian Epstein's house?' I said. 'Yes, sir,' he said,
and led the way to the hall. I suddenly realised that the man
was the butler. I've never seen one before . . . He took me into
a room and said in a loud voice 'Mr Orton'. Everybody looked
up and stood to their feet. I was introduced to one or two
people. And Paul McCartney. He was just as the photographs.
Only he'd grown a moustache. His hair was shorter too. He
was playing the latest Beatles record 'Penny Lane'. I like it
very much. Then he played the other side — Strawberry
something. I didn't like this as much. We talked intermittently.
Before we went out to dinner we agreed to throw out the idea
of setting the film in the thirties. We went down to dinner. The
trusted old retainer — looking too much like a butler to be
good casting — busied himself in the corner. 'The only thing I
get from the theatre,' Paul M. said, 'is a sore arse.' He said
Loot was the only play he hadn't wanted to leave before the
end. 'I'd've liked a bit more,' he said. We talked of the theatre.
I said that compared with the pop-scene the theatre was square.
'The theatre started going down hill when Queen Victoria
knighted Henry Irving,' I said. 'Too fucking respectable'. We

talked of drugs, of mushrooms which give hallucinations — like L.S.D. 'The drug not the money,' I said. We talked of tattoos. And after one or two veiled references, marijuana. I said I'd smoked it in Morocco. The atmosphere relaxed a little. Dinner ended and we went upstairs agains. We watched a programme on TV; it had phrases in it like 'the in crowd' and 'swinging London'. There was a little scratching at the door. I thought it was the old retainer, but someone got up to open the door and about five very young and pretty boys trouped in. I rather hoped this was the evening's entertainment. It wasn't, though. It was a pop group called The Easybeats. I'd seen them on TV. I liked them very much . . . A French photographer arrived . . . He'd taken a set of new photographs of The Beatles. They wanted one to use on the record sleeve. Excellent photographs. The four Beatles look different in their moustaches. Like anarchists in the early years of the century. After a while . . . I talked to the leading Easybeat. Feeling slightly like an Edwardian masher with a Gaiety girl. And then I came over tired and decided to go home. I had a last word with Paul M. 'Well,' I said, 'I'd like to do the film. There's only one thing we've got to fix up.' 'You mean the bread?' 'Yes'. We smiled and parted. I got a cab home. Told Kenneth about it. Then he got up to make a cup of tea. And we talked a little more. And went to sleep.

While the contract was being negotiated (£5,000 for the first draft with the right to buy the script back if unacceptable to the Beatles), Orton grew a moustache and blithely got to work. 'I shall enjoy writing the film,' he wrote in his diary.

Orton worked fast, aided by the discovery — 'inspiration' was his word for it — of an old novel which provided the backbone of the scenario. 'I'd already written the beginning of the script up to where McTurk is thrown out of town,' he wrote on January 29. 'And then I remembered that in the cupboard somewhere was the manuscript of a novel I'd written in 1959 called THE VISION OF GOMBOLD PROVAL [posthumously published as *Head To Toe*]. It had always been my intention some day to rewrite it. I decided to get it down and see if there was anything I could use. I found, to my surprise, that it was excellent. It has great faults as a novel, but as the basis for a film it was more than adequate. So I'm rewriting the whole thing. Miraculously towards the middle of the novel four young men appear.' By February 11, when Orton was summoned to Shenson's office for one final pep talk before the contract was signed, the script was almost completed.

Shenson 'was most concerned to impress me that "the boys" shouldn't be made to do anything in the film that would reflect badly on them,' Orton wrote, getting his first dose of the screen-writer's second debilitating hazard: the commercial compromise. 'You see, he said, 'the kids will all imitate whatever the boys do.' I hadn't the heart to tell him that the boys, in my script, have been caught in flagrante, become involved in dubious political activity, dressed as women, committed murder, been put in prison and committed adultery. And the script isn't finished yet. I thought it best to say nothing of my plans for the Beatles until he had a chance of reading the script. We parted at five o'clock amicably. With the contract, according to him, as good as signed. And on my part, the film almost written.'

Even in its title, *Up Against It* announced the rambunctious sexuality of Orton's trickster temperament. Phallic fun was part of his comic revenge on society. In his life and his work, Orton displayed a trickster's ruthless sexual rapacity. He wanted to goose an audience and take it for a tumble. He was a hostile sharpshooter loudly proclaiming his innocence. But his diaries leave no doubt about the anarchic prupose behind his outrageous-ness:

> Kenneth, who reads the *Observer*, tells me of the latest group thing in America — complete sexual licence. 'It's the only way to smash the wretched civilisation', I said, making a mental note to hot-up *What the Butler Saw* when I rewrite . . . Sex is the only way to infuriate them. Much more fucking and they'll be screaming hysterics in next to no time.

Orton had learned how to corrupt an audience with pleasure. It was a rare gift, and one that had not come easy. 'Cleanse my heart, give me the ability to rage correctly,' prays Gombold, Orton's spokesman in *Head to Toe*. But it took a six month prison term for the comic defacement of public library books in 1962 to bring a saving detachment to his writing. He had dreamed of a cauterising verbal power that would create a 'seismic distur-bance'. In time, he found a way to make language stir things up. His lethal wit conjured up the same wicked and faithless world that had always enraged him, but with a difference. It made his anger irresistible. *Up Against It* signals the new playfulness that came with Orton's liberation from anonymity and self-doubt. Bitterness had evaporated from his writing to be replaced by a detached gaiety at the murderous vanity of mankind.

LOW. I'm hungry. I need help.
MRS O'SCULLION. I'm not interested in your private life.

Always the enemy of boundaries, Orton played havoc not only
with society's notions of normality but the literary genres that
codified it. *Up Against It* attempts to do to movie romance what
Loot had done to detective fiction and *What the Butler Saw*
would do to classical farce. The film uses romantic imagery while
the dialogue takes pot-shots at the assumptions beneath it.

LOW. Is there any woman you wouldn't wait in the rain for?
McTURK. The Statue of Liberty.

All the romantic ideals — devotion, loyalty, monogamy — are
turned upside down as Orton attempts to invent a new form
while satirising the old one. *Up Against It* teases the cosy, lustless
screen version of romance. 'Anything worth doing, is worth doing
in public', McTurk observes. In their outrageousness, the
characters are always commenting on the courtly romantic setting.
'I must go,' Rowena says to McTurk, shafting him yet again in
the last minutes of the film. 'Love seems out of place in a garden
in the moonlight.' McTurk finds solace in the arms of a second
woman who has unsuccessfully pursued him throughout the film.
'My heart is broken', he tells Patricia Drumgoole, about to propose
marriage as Orton lampoons the romantic equation of suffering
with satisfaction. 'But everything else is in working order.' After
their adventures, the characters are more pragmatic about life.
The marriage takes place — a happy ending in which romantic
propaganda is mischievously inverted so that the bride can have
three bridegrooms. 'Just the happy quartette', coos the photographer snapping the new marriage of Love, Money and Lust
on the steps of the church. The third husband is a rebel leader
who sees marriage as a radical act. 'Getting married and having
children is the most rebellious thing a man can do', says Jack
Ramsay. 'It shows a disregard for the conventional bourgeois
status quo and a fine, careless anarchic sense of the absurd.'
Marriage, which institutionalises the sexual scarcity romance
promotes, gives way in the film's final image to a vision of sexual
abundance:

> The young men kiss her. There is a struggle. MISS DRUM-
> GOOLE squeals with delight and disappears under the
> coverlet with her husbands.

THE END

'Oscar Lewenstein read *Up Against It* and liked it very much', Orton wrote on February 25, a day after he'd handed in his first draft. 'He thought it had a poetic quality. This is because I used all the romantic clichés — moonlight, roses, unrequited love and the Cinderella figure of the poor girl who loves him and is finally rewarded by his love in the last reel. O.L. said he liked least the scenes in the Albert Hall (with the shooting of the woman Prime Minister Lillian Corbett). This clearly because of the parody of the Kennedy assassination he doesn't think that Epstein, The Beatles, or W. Shenson will opt for it.'

But it was panic, not poetry, that the script explored. *Up Against It* is part of Orton's experiment in farce method, his search for a way to marry terror and elation. 'I'm Princess of the Church', says the Archbishop of Canterbury who turns out to be a woman in Orton's parody of the Sidney Street Siege. 'Let me pass. I've some hard praying to do.' Violating social and familial pieties, the upheavals of farce created the shock Orton wanted in laughter. In its pandemonium, farce provided him with the perfect anarchist apocalypse. Orton tried to show this in his battle scene where McTurk, Low and Ramsay run their ambulance into an enemy truck and start a chain reaction of destruction from which no one emerges victorious. Nothing can diminish the panorama of suffering. Every heroic gesture turns into a fiasco. 'The victims and the helpers struggle together in the mud of the battlefield'. Orton even produces the final abyss which engulfs everyone.

Mayhem is Orton's metaphor for history: a tableau of viciousness in which to be saved from one disaster is only to be eligible for greater violence. 'Seeing what has happened before. [McTurk, Low and Ramsay] decline to be helped and fight off the stretcher bearers.' The victims become victimisers in a struggle to cling to life and remain intact.

When a priest and choir boys appear on the scene, the promise of salvation in the midst of carnage floors the rebels. Low, 'struck dumb, kneels'. McTurk, overcome by despair, 'bursts into tears and fits of sobbing'. But Ramsay 'shrieks with maniacal laughter and begins to leap about in a kind of glee'. Orton would choose the latter course. His grotesque laughter rejected the impotence of despair.

'I've just got McTurk in prison', Orton wrote on February 26, and realise, of course, the whole script is about schizophrenia'. Like Orton, the characters teeter between optimism and disenchantment, rebellion and acceptance, male and female roles.

Farce becomes a paradigm for the tumult of consciousness. 'Back! Back to the women! Our only hope!' pleads one character, grabbing the steering wheel of a car as McTurk and Low try to change allegiance from the all-female goverment troops to the male rebels. The driver replies: 'No! The men! We must go on.'

Orton had written *Up Against It* so fast that he asked Peggy Ramsay to wait three weeks before submitting it. She found the script 'splendid', although, as Orton noted in his diary, 'she was worried by the way what she called my "dubious morality" showed through. Especially the killing of the Prime Minister.' The script was sent to Shenson on March 6. 'Peggy feels it will be too much for him,' Orton wrote in his diary. She was right. He called the next day, saying he was 'fascinated' but worried whether it should be four boys or four aspects of one person.

'. . . As you know, Joe, we're all different people. And we have to learn to live with those aspects. I understand that the original idea was to show how a man can live with himself.' Which is pretentious shit. I can't write that, or, what is more important, alter my script to fit that idea. I'd much rather have it about four boys anyway. Shenson is going to speak to Epstein from Los Angeles tonight. He has suggested Antonioni to direct. Rubbish!

By March 29, Orton had still heard nothing from the Beatles. He fixed on Brian Epstein as the culprit: 'An amateur and a fool. He isn't equipped to judge the quality of a script. Probably he will never say "yes" equally hasn't got the courage to say "no". A thoroughly weak, flaccid type.' And then on April 4, *Up Against It* was returned. 'No explanation why. No criticism of the script. And apparently, Brian Epstein has no comment to make either. Fuck them.'

But Orton's luck was still holding. On April 10, the day the *Evening Standard* reported 'the shock of Joe Orton's pride', he was revising *Up Against It* for Oscar Lewenstein. 'I've turned the four Beatles into three young men. It's a much better script without the weight of stars hanging on it.' [It is this revised script which is printed here.] Two days later, Lewenstein bought it for £10,000 and 10% of the production company's net profits − an altogether better deal than the Beatles had offered. Lewenstein, who as director of Woodfall Productions had been associated with *Tom Jones, A Taste of Honey, The Loneliness of the Long Distance Runner* and many other high quality productions in the short-lived British cinema renaissance, thought *Up Against It* 'probably the best first draft of a screen-play I have ever read.' For his part, Orton was delighted. He had just sold *Loot* to the movies for a reported £100,000 and was re-writing *The Erpingham Camp* and *The Ruffian on the Stair* for a double bill called *Crimes of Passion* at the Royal Court in June. He had every reason to feel merry and to swagger to an American friend: 'I'm now engaged on a film for which I'm being paid the equivalent of $30,000. I'm going up, up, up.'

'To be young, good-looking, healthy, famous, comparatively rich *and* happy is surely going against nature,' Orton wrote in his diary on May 22. He and Halliwell were talking about how happy they were in Morocco and worrying that perhaps they were too happy and 'would be struck down from afar by disaster.' On that day Orton wrote: 'I hope no doom strikes'. Ten weeks later, they were dead. On August 9, 1967, a chauffeur sent to drive Orton to Twickenham Studios to discuss *Up Against It* with Richard Lester, discovered the bodies in their Islington bedsitter. Halliwell had battered in Orton's head with a hammer, and then swallowed twenty-two Nembutals to kill himself. In their writing together, Orton and Halliwell had imagined everything about their relationship except success. And Orton's success only magnified Halliwell's punishing sense of failure and put Orton out of touch with his friend's suffering. Through murder, Halliwell achieved the public association with Joe Orton's career that he'd been denied in life.

Oscar Lewenstein put other playwrights to work on *Up Against It*. Charles Wood, James Saunders, Roger McGough, and Christopher Logue all tinkered with the script. But the wicked fun Orton poked at the world was inimitable; and the film was finally abandoned. The script remains a tantalising remnant of what might have been, the last comic fragment of a voluptuary of fiasco.

John Lahr

John Lahr is the author of *Prick Up Your Ears*: The Biography of Joe Orton.

CAST LIST

(Main characters only)

IAN McTURK
CHRISTOPHER LOW
JACK RAMSAY
FATHER BRODIE
THE MAYOR
MISS DRUMGOOLE
CONNIE
ROWENA TORRENCE
MRS O'SCULLION
BERNARD COATES
RAMSAY'S FATHER

1. Exterior. A city. *Unreal in the light of the setting sun. Smoke drifts from a chimney. A bell is heard from a church tower. Children call. A sudden silence.*

2. Exterior. A deserted street. Evening. *A church against the sky. Next to the church a large house standing in an unweeded garden. Laurels and rhododendrons in the watery light.*

3. Exterior. The roof of the house. Evening. *A cat crosses the tiles to the edge of a skylight. A bedroom is seen through the skylight. A bed with a candlewick bedspread. On the bed a GIRL is lying. She has her face buried in the pillow. She is sobbing.*

4. Interior. The bedroom. *On a table beside the bed is a photograph of a young man (IAN McTURK). The girl, (ROWENA TORRENCE) sits up. She wipes her eyes, lifts the photograph from the table. Stares at it. Kisses it. Weeps.*

5. Interior. A stairwell from above. *At the bottom of the well, in the hall, IAN McTURK and CHRISTOPHER LOW are sitting. Their arms are folded across their chests. They are wearing dark suits and ties.*

6. Interior. Father Brodie's study. *Brown leather chairs. Bookcases full of musty books. A faded carpet on the floor. A large desk. A green-shaded lamp. FATHER BRODIE is sitting at his desk. A man (the MAYOR) and a woman (CONNIE) are in the room with FATHER BRODIE. CONNIE wears a police uniform. FATHER BRODIE pours a whisky. MISS DRUMGOOLE enters from the hall. She is a kind, rather plain girl. She wears a starched apron.*

MISS DRUMGOOLE. The young men are outside, sir. They're in a repentant mood. Don't be too hard on them.

FATHER BRODIE. The matter is out of my hands, Miss Drumgoole. Such wickedness cannot be tolerated. Ask them to step this way.

MISS DRUMGOOLE *shakes her head. She goes out.*
FATHER BRODIE *lifts a figure of a praying saint. It is hollow.*
He fits it over, and conceals the whisky bottle.

7. Interior. The corridor. McTURK *and* LOW *are waiting. Their arms are folded.* MISS DRUMGOOLE *appears in the doorway.*

MISS DRUMGOOLE. Father Brodie will see you now. He's been wrestling all afternoon with his conscience.

McTURK. Who won?

MISS DRUMGOOLE. You must ask him yourself. It's not a question a girl like me can put to a priest.

She leads the way into the study.

8. Interior. Father Brodie's study. McTURK *and* LOW *are shown in by* MISS DRUMGOOLE.

FATHER BRODIE. Come in. Close the door quietly. My choirboys are asleep.

LOW *shuts the door. He and* McTURK *stand before the desk.* MISS DRUMGOOLE *folds her hands together by the bookcase. The others in the room regard the two young men with a sour expression.*

MAYOR (*standing to his feet*). We've been deputed to act as spokesmen for the citizens of this town. I believe you've already met Father Brodie, priest of this Parish and one-time heckler at Orange rallies?

FATHER BRODIE *acknowledges the compliment with a gracious smile. The* MAYOR *turns to* CONNIE.

MAYOR. And this is Police Superintendant Constance Boon — to rhyme, most appropriately with Loon. As you know I am Terence O'Scullion, Lord Mayor and prominent right-wing politician. I also hold strong views on sexual promiscuity and the taking of drugs.

FATHER BRODIE. Do you object to Miss Drumgoole being present at this interview?

McTURK. No. She's been a real friend to us. Through all the troubles we've endured since we came to this town.

MISS DRUMGOOLE *weeps silently. The* MAYOR *turns to the young men and speaks in a cold, unemotional tone.*

MAYOR. The townsfolk won't tolerate any longer your indiscretions. They have recently, with the destruction of the Memorial to the Fallen of two world wars, reached monumental proportions.

LOW. We weren't responsible for blowing up the War Memorial, sir. I've always been against such pointless anarchy.

MAYOR. Who then d'you suggest damaged a monument which cost ten thousand pounds?

FATHER BRODIE. In 1919.

MAYOR. It would be worth considerably more today. Why, the allegorical figure of Peace, even without her left arm, must be quite valuable. And you say that you weren't responsible?

McTURK. No.

CONNIE. You were seen by a constable to place a large wreath at the foot of the monument. Shortly afterwards the wreath exploded. Do you deny that you mined the Flanders poppies in that wreath?

LOW. I met a man by the Corn Exchange. He said he was a World War Two veteran. He pressed the wreath into my hands, begging me to place it under the bronze plaque to his fallen comrades. This I did. Shortly afterwards the Memorial was shaken by a violent explosion. I had nothing whatever to do with the outrage. I placed the wreath there in order to help a sick man.

CONNIE. Never, in the whole of my life, have I heard anything so lame and stupid!

FATHER BRODIE. I shall add insolence to the list of misdemeanours for which you're to be punished. (*He makes a note in a folder on his desk.*) Sit down.

McTURK *lowers himself into a chair.*

FATHER BRODIE. Not on that chair. It has a broken leg.

McTURK. Have you sent for a doctor?

FATHER BRODIE. Doctors can do nothing for it. It's incurable.

LOW. What about faith healing?

FATHER BRODIE. I've no faith in faith healing.

The two young men sit on an ottoman.

FATHER BRODIE. I won't waste more time discussing your conduct. I'll come straight to the point. At four a.m. this morning my own niece, Rowena Torrence, was seen to enter your room in an advanced state of nudity. What excuse had she for being with you at that hour?

McTURK. She'd come to borrow a cup of sugar.

CONNIE. But she's on a diet.

McTURK. I didn't give in to her demands.

MAYOR. Was she provocative?

McTURK. Nobody is provocative at four in the morning.

FATHER BRODIE. A woman's wiles are in operation at any hour of the day or night. (*With a cough.*) So I've heard.

LOW. Well, Father, I've had less experience of women than you. I've always led a decent life.

McTURK. It wasn't me who let your niece into the room, Father.

FATHER BRODIE. That isn't true. I saw the incident with my own eyes. (*To* CONNIE.) Do you confirm that, Superintendant?

CONNIE. I handed you the binoculars myself, Father.

MAYOR. And you left the blind up as well, McTurk. The last indulgence of a sensualist.

FATHER BRODIE. It's my painful duty to have to inform you, McTurk, that my niece, upon careful scrutiny, appears to be as much in need of repair as the Memorial to the Fallen. For your outrage upon the living and for your friend's outrage upon the dead the City Fathers have decided to expel you both from this fair city.

MISS DRUMGOOLE *gives a cry.*

MISS DRUMGOOLE (*to the young men*). What's to become of you both now?

FATHER BRODIE. You'll meet the Lord Mayor and the Aldermen tomorrow morning. They will escort you to the city limits.

McTURK. Can't I see Rowena? To say goodbye. I love her very much.

LOW. It seems a pity not to return her cup of sugar.

FATHER BRODIE. My niece is confined to her room. I've forbidden her to communicate with anybody. (*To* MISS DRUMGOOLE.) Show them the door. I've business to discuss with the Lord Mayor.

MISS DRUMGOOLE *opens the door.* McTURK *and* LOW *follow her.* FATHER BRODIE *lifts the praying saint from the whisky bottle.*

9. Interior. The corridor. MISS DRUMGOOLE *enters followed by the two young men.* MISS DRUMGOOLE *leads the way to the door.*

MISS DRUMGOOLE. I shall miss our evening walks to the public library. Who will carry my books now?

LOW. We're innocent of everything. I feel like crying when I think of all I've had to endure.

McTURK (*to* MISS DRUMGOOLE). Will you give a message to Miss Torrence?

MISS DRUMGOOLE *turns quickly. Stares at him in horror.*

MISS DRUMGOOLE. Father Brodie would be dreadfully upset if he knew I'd betrayed his trust.

McTURK. I'll be in the garden.

MISS DRUMGOOLE *shakes her head. Opens the front door.*

MISS DRUMGOOLE. There was a time when I thought you loved me, Ian McTurk. You brought me flowers and boxes of inexpensive chocolates. Now all you can think of is the lovely Rowena Torrence. She has stolen you from me.

It is raining outside. The sun has set. A cold wind is blowing.

MISS DRUMGOOLE. I should hate her, but I can't. She's so beautiful. (*With a wistful sigh.*) I'll tell her you're in the garden.

McTURK *kisses her ardently. He releases her.* McTURK *and* LOW *go into the garden.* MISS DRUMGOOLE *shuts the door.*

MISS DRUMGOOLE (*with an ecstatic shiver*). Ian McTurk gives a most charming sensation when he kisses. I understand how he sets all hearts aflame!

10. Exterior. The shrubbery at the back of the house. Night.
The boys push their way through dank and dripping rhododendrons. Rain streams down their faces.

LOW. Oh, if only I hadn't offered to help that El Alamein veteran carry his wreath, I'd've been home in time to prevent you taking the virginity of Father Brodie's niece. My kind heart has undone us both.

McTURK. Yes, you must learn to control your generous impulses.

LOW. If we're caught speaking to Miss Torrence we'll be in trouble. Let's leave this place at once.

McTURK. I must say goodbye. Rowena is the most beautiful and the most cultured girl I've ever met. She speaks three languages and she's an expert conjuror. She's worth waiting in the rain for.

LOW. Is there any woman you wouldn't wait in the rain for?

McTURK. The Statue of Liberty.

They push on through the shrubs. The rain streams down their faces.

11. Exterior. A balcony overlooking the shrubbery. ROWENA TORRENCE *comes onto the balcony carrying an umbrella. She is wearing a nightgown.* MISS DRUMGOOLE *appears behind her in the lighted window.*

MISS DRUMGOOLE. Hurry with your last goodbyes, Miss Rowena. Your uncle wishes to speak to you.

ROWENA. What for?

MISS DRUMGOOLE. He's sending you to a convent. You'll be in safe hands there, he says. All the nuns are women.

ROWENA (*looking about her into the rain*). Oh, my darling, where are you?

She comes forward onto the balcony with the umbrella. Speaks her words to the night and the sighing branches.

ROWENA. My heart is breaking. I'll never see him again!

The rain is lashed to a fury by the wind. McTURK *and* LOW *appear through the bushes. Their clothes are sticking to them with rain. They wave.*

McTURK. We've been ordered to leave the town. Will you be there to see us off?

ROWENA. No.

McTURK. Why not?

ROWENA. I'm being sent away too.

MISS DRUMGOOLE (*appearing on the balcony*). Your uncle is coming. Hurry unless you want him to catch you.

ROWENA. There's no pain like the pain of first love. (*With a cry of anguish.*) I shall remember the heartbreak of this moment for ever!

She leans over the balcony. McTURK *climbs onto* LOW's *shoulders.* McTURK *kisses* ROWENA. MISS DRUMGOOLE *pulls her away.* ROWENA *hurries into the house.*

MISS DRUMGOOLE. Away with you, Ian McTurk. Your wild ways will bring nothing but harm.

McTURK (*urgently*). Can I write to her? What's her address?

MISS DRUMGOOLE. She can be reached c/o Mrs O'Scullion, The Convent of La Dulcinella, 42 Millfield Street, Bradford.

She hurries indoors. McTURK *and* LOW *push their way into the shrubbery.* MISS DRUMGOOLE *reappears on the balcony.*

MISS DRUMGOOLE (*calling*). And kindly mark your letters 'Secular'.

12. Exterior. The shrubbery. McTURK *and* LOW *pushing through the dripping bushes.*

McTURK. I feel numb at the thought of losing her.

LOW. She didn't do any conjuring tricks.

They push on.

LOW. She leans well over a balcony, though. For a woman.

13. Exterior. The front of the house. Night. *The two young men approach the edge of the shrubbery and step onto the drive.* FATHER BRODIE *opens the front door and shouts to them.*

FATHER BRODIE. Unless you leave these premises at once, I'll set the dog onto you!

> *They stuff their hands into their pockets and hurry away from the house.*

14. Exterior. A main thoroughfare of the city. Early morning. *Weak sunlight. A light breeze blowing. A procession of citizens. Slow march. Music. Drum and cymbals.*

At the head of the procession is FATHER BRODIE. *Six* CHORISTERS *surround him. They swing censers and chant a solemn dirge.*

The MAYOR (TERENCE O'SCULLION) *and the* LADY MAYORESS (MRS O'SCULLION) *in their robes of office, lead the* ALDERMEN *and* CIVIC DIGNITARIES.

McTURK *and* LOW *are escorted by* CONNIE *and a number of* MOUNTED POLICEMEN *and* WOMEN.

Banners, billowing in the early breeze, are carried by WOMEN. 'I fell under his fatal spell', 'I was happy till I met Ian McTurk', 'He ruined my life'.

Members of the BRITISH LEGION *and ex-Servicemen's associations carry banners:* 'Hands off public monuments', 'Hang him!' 'Hooligans out!' *and* 'Did we die for this?'.

The procession passes, leaving MISS DRUMGOOLE *alone in the street. She watches the procession disappear and dabs her eyes.*

MISS DRUMGOOLE. What's to become of them now? (*Puts away her handkerchief.*) Whatever they've done they have kind hearts. I love them both, but Ian McTurk is my special favourite.

> *She gives way to a fresh burst of tears.*

MISS DRUMGOOLE. How shall I ever bear not seeing his cheery smile every morning?

> *She blows her nose and makes her way up the street.*

15. Exterior. Scrubland. Distant houses. *The sun has risen higher. The procession approaches. The music stops. The procession halts. Silence.*

The MOUNTED POLICEWOMEN *lead* McTURK *and* LOW *forward.* FATHER BRODIE, CONNIE *and the* MAYOR *follow them to a signpost which says* 'You are now entering the city limits. We hope your stay will be pleasant'.

The POLICEWOMEN, *the* PRISONERS, CONNIE, FATHER BRODIE *and the* MAYOR *stop by the signpost.* FATHER BRODIE *takes a book from his pocket.*

FATHER BRODIE. Here is a copy of the scriptures. I've marked the relevant passages on Charity, Brotherly Love and the consuming of unlawful meat. Take them to your heart and your future lives will be blameless.

LOW (*accepting the book*). It was me who dropped the hair lacquer into the font, Father, I can't leave without making a clean breast of it.

FATHER BRODIE. Don't mention breasts in my presence. I'm a celibate.

He steps back. The MAYOR *steps forward.*

MAYOR. In order that you shan't be able to claim that we cast you adrift without means, the citizens present you with this wallet. (*Applause from the crowd.*) In it is twenty pounds and a photograph of the new wing of the Maternity Home.

McTURK *accepts the wallet.*

McTURK. I'm rather surprised that you should consider building a new wing to the Maternity Home now, sir. It'll be empty when I've gone.

MAYOR. I think you'd better leave that particular problem to me, McTurk. I'm not a man to see a Maternity Home empty for long.

He steps back. CONNIE *steps forward.*

CONNIE. You've heard what Father Brodie and the Lord Mayor have to say to you. And now, get out of the town! We never wish to see you again.

The citizens boo loudly, and wave their banners. McTURK *and* LOW *turn and walk away. The gap between the citizens and the two boys widens.*

16. Exterior. A piece of rising ground. *The citizens dwarfed on the horizon. The boys top the ridge. They turn back to look. The procession dips its banners and melts away.*

A vast and chequered plain lies ahead. In the distance is a dark forest. McTURK *and* LOW *loosen their collars and strike out into the unknown world that lies waiting.*

McTURK. We're free!

LOW. On our own!

McTURK. The world's our oyster!

LOW. The bad times have gone. Happiness lies ahead!

17. Exterior. A dark forest. Evening. *Silence. The two young men, footsore and weary, push their way through the undergrowth. A* MAN's *voice is heard calling for help.* LOW *stops.*

LOW. What's that?

McTURK (*without stopping*). Someone's calling for help. Haven't you heard the sound of a fellow human being in distress before?

LOW. No.

McTURK. It's replaced 'Sweet Lavender' as a street cry.

LOW. Let's see what's the matter?

He turns back. McTURK *seizes him by the hand.*

McTURK. Remember the old soldier and his wreath? Curb this insatiable desire to offer a helping hand. It'll bring you nothing but unhappiness.

LOW. I must see what they want.

He shrugs McTURK *away. He starts off into the undergrowth in the direction of the cries for help.*

McTURK (*shouting after him*). Remember what happened when you helped the old lady across the road? She beat you senseless with her umbrella.

LOW *stops. Half turns.*

LOW (*to himself*). She'd just come out of hospital.

McTURK (*catching up with him*). You occupied the bed she'd just left for a month.

> LOW *moves off again.* McTURK *catches his arm.*

McTURK. What about the blind man who you gave your last shilling to? He nearly bit your finger off.

LOW. He had a nervous nature.

> *He pushes on through the undergrowth.* McTURK *shrugs. Turns back to the path. Leaves* LOW. LOW *goes on alone.*

18. Exterior. Another part of the forest. Night. McTURK *is nowhere in sight.* LOW *pushes his way through the thick undergrowth. The cries for help are near at hand. He stops before a hole in the ground. He stares. By the rim of the hole in the ground is a pie dish. A half-empty jar of pickles. A cheese, a fork and asparagus tongs, a coffee pot, a box of biscuits and a decanter.* LOW *looks down the hole.*

19. Interior. Down the hole. *A* MAN *is standing at the bottom of the hole. He is fat. He has a bald head. He stares up at* LOW.

LOW. D'you want any help?

FAT MAN. Have you got a rope?

LOW. No.

FAT MAN. You'll find one on the path. I'd be grateful if you'd hurry. There isn't much time.

20. Exterior. The forest. A few yards from the hole. LOW *is looking for a rope. A man is seen approaching on a white horse. He has a kindly expression on his face. He is shabbily dressed. He is about forty years of age. His name is* BERNARD COATES. *As the horse approaches* LOW *runs up to* BERNARD COATES.

LOW (*politely*). You don't happen to have a rope on you, sir?

> *Without a moment's thought* BERNARD COATES *slashes at* LOW *with his riding crop and continues his journey.* LOW *gives a cry of pain and fright. He puts a hand to his cheek*

which is bleeding. He stumbles off the path and, in doing so, discovers a rope lying at the foot of a tree.

21. Exterior. The hole. LOW *is pulling the* FAT MAN *from the hole. The man's face appears over the rim. His body appears. Finally he crawls from his prison.* LOW *blows on his hands which are cut and scraped by the rope.*

LOW (*with a pleasant smile*). Have you been down there long?

> *The man says nothing. He seizes* LOW *by the throat with one hand and pummels him with the other.* LOW *is too surprised to resist. The* FAT MAN *drags him, nearly senseless, to the rim of the hole.* LOW *cries out in anguish.*
> *On the edge of the hole the* FAT MAN *pauses. He is about to fling* LOW *down into the prison when the bushes in front of them part and* BERNARD COATES *appears. He is on foot. Seeing the struggle taking place by the hole he runs forward and separates the combatants. As* LOW *draws back from his attacker,* BERNARD COATES *begins to beat the* FAT MAN *about the face and body. Ignoring the man's cries of distress, he hurls him back into the hole.* LOW, *nursing his wounds, is too surprised by what has taken place to say anything.*
> BERNARD COATES *collects the food lying beside the hole. He puts it into a bag which he has with him. As he does so, he addresses* LOW, *over his shoulder.*

COATES. What are you doing in this forest? It isn't common land, you know.

LOW. I heard someone calling for help and came to their rescue.

> BERNARD COATES *stops. Stares hard at* LOW.

COATES. What right had you to do such a thing? Are you a member of the Women's Voluntary Service?

LOW. No.

COATES. Then your action was misguided and uncalled-for.

> *He picks up his bag and walks away. As he does so* LOW *calls after him.*

LOW. How do I get out of this forest? I'm lost.

> *Without turning round or stopping* BERNARD COATES *answers him.*

COATES. You can come with me if you wish. I own vast tracts of the land around here. I'm a millionaire.

LOW (*following him*). Why was that man down the hole? Is he a prisoner?

COATES. Of course he's a prisoner. I should've thought that was obvious.

LOW. What've you done with your horse?

COATES. It threw me as I was crossing a stream. I shall have it destroyed. I've no time to waste on dumb animals. Yet I've a kindly nature. You'd be surprised how generous I can be. You can carry my bag if you like. I'm a man with a charitable nature.

He hands his bag to LOW *who shoulders it.*

22. Exterior. A clearing in the forest. LOW *and* BERNARD COATES *are sitting under a tree. They are eating food from* BERNARD's *bag.*

COATES. My name is Bernard Coates. I'm very rich and I'm engaged to be married. You probably find that hard to believe?

LOW. No.

COATES. I suppose you think I couldn't be rich because I have such bad teeth?

LOW. If you're so rich why can't you afford a shilling for a toothbrush?

COATES. I have bad teeth because if you're rich it doesn't matter whether you disgust people or not. In fact I'll go as far as to say that the poor prefer the rich to be disgusting.

He crams a piece of pie into his mouth. He almost chokes. LOW pats him on the back.

COATES (*wiping his mouth*). Are you rich? I'd be surprised if you were.

LOW. I haven't got a penny to bless myself with.

COATES. That must be most inconvenient for you. Would you like to go to a party?

LOW. Yes.

COATES. Let me just bury the remains of this food and I'll take you to one.

He gets up and is soon lost among the trees.

23. Exterior. The same spot. Later. *An owl hoots.* LOW *wanders in search of* BERNARD COATES.

LOW (*calling, anxious*). Bernard! Bernard Coates! (*Pause.*) Where are you?

No reply. He stumbles along the path. He is soon lost among the trees.

24. Exterior. Another part of the forest. McTURK *is sitting wrapped in his overcoat. A chill mist has fallen over the forest.* LOW *approaches across the clearing. He is weary, his face is stained with blood. He whistles tunelessly between his teeth.*

McTURK. Who roughed you up?

LOW. A man I tried to help. (*He limps toward* McTURK.) I'll never do another generous act as long as I live.

McTURK. You've said that before. You always revert.

25. Exterior. A stone gateway leading into the drive of a small manor house. Early morning. *A ornamental iron plaque swings over the gate. It says:* 'MONEY-BOX LODGE'.
McTURK *and* LOW *approach the gate.*

LOW. This house looks promising. Let's ask for food.

McTURK. No. I'm too proud to beg.

LOW. We could pay with the money that the Lord Mayor gave us.

McTURK *takes the wallet from his pocket. He opens it. He realises with surprise and misgiving, that it is empty.*

LOW. What's happened to the money?

McTURK. There never was any money. The Mayor's speech was made with half an eye to the local elections. I'd rather starve than enter a house like this.

He trudges away, proud and lonely. LOW shrugs, walks up the drive.

26. Exterior. *LOW approaches the front door of Money-Box Lodge. He searches for a bell. He can't find one. He pushes the door open. He goes inside.*

27. Interior. The hall of Money-Box Lodge. *A balcony runs the length of one wall. A wide staircase leads from it. LOW finds his feet sinking into the rich pile of the carpet. He stops. Silence. A door on the landing opens and BERNARD COATES appears dressed in his underclothes. He carries a folded newspaper.*

LOW (*calling to* BERNARD COATES). Might I have a word with you, sir.

    BERNARD COATES stops, sees who is calling him, is extremely agitated. He comes down the stairs and puts a jaunty expression on his face in order to conceal his real feelings.

COATES (*waving the newspaper*). The election results are through. (*With a breezy smile.*) Had you heard the news?

LOW. I'm too tired to bother with them.

COATES. Well you can borrow my paper. I've finished with it now.

    He pushes the newspaper into LOW's hand and hurries away with a nervous smile. LOW is left alone. He opens the newspaper.

28. Front page of the paper. *A photograph of a smiling woman, microphones before her. A man lifting her hand in victory. Caption says:* 'LILLY CORBETT IT IS!'

29. *LOW opens the newspaper at an inside page.*

30. Close-up of inside page. *Headline:* 'A DELIGHTFULLY FEMININE PRIME MINISTER!'

31. Interior. The hall. *LOW folds up the newspaper. A tall, well-built WOMAN appears in a doorway opposite him. LOW smiles.*

LOW. Are you the owner of the house?

The woman (MRS O'SCULLION) *points a gun at him.*

MRS O'SCULLION. Stay where you are! Don't attempt to
escape or I shall have no hesitation in shooting you.

LOW. I'm hungry and thirsty. I need help.

MRS O'SCULLION. I'm not interested in your private life. What
are you doing here?

LOW. I found the door open. I meant no harm.

MRS O'SCULLION. Who gave you permission to read that
paper? It's private property, you know. Put it down.

LOW *puts the newspaper onto a table.* BERNARD COATES
appears in the doorway.

LOW (*seeing* BERNARD *with relief*). I met you last night, sir.
Don't you remember? You promised to take me to a party.

BERNARD COATES *glances at* MRS O'SCULLION *with
apprehension. Looks back at* LOW. *Gives a little cough of
apology.*

COATES. There's no party here. You'll have to go somewhere
else.

MRS O'SCULLION (*to* COATES). Why are you talking to strange
young men without your trousers?

COATES. I was dressing for dinner. This fellow came and asked
me to take him to a party.

MRS O'SCULLION *casts a withering glance at* BERNARD
COATES.

MRS O'SCULLION. It was premature to take your clothes off.
He's obviously a burglar.

BERNARD COATES *nods to* LOW *and shambles away up the
stairs.* MRS O'SCULLION *calls into another room.*

MRS O'SCULLION. Con! Where are you! Give us a hand.

CONNIE *appears. She has on a pair of men's pyjamas and a
plaid dressing-gown. She stands for a moment taking in the
situation.*

MRS O'SCULLION. This kid forced his way in here and wants
Bernie to take him to a party.

CONNIE *turns to* LOW. *There is an ironical contempt for him in the way she looks him up and down. She waves* MRS O'SCULLION *aside.* MRS O'SCULLION *puts the gun away.*

CONNIE (*to* LOW). Where's your friend?

LOW. He's gone ahead. I came in here for help.

CONNIE (*coming closer*). You're an attractive little thing, aren't you? (*She puts a hand under his chin.*) You're not frightened of me, are you?

LOW. Yes.

CONNIE (*to* MRS O'SCULLION). Give him a room.

MRS O'SCULLION's *mouth drops open in amazement.*

MRS O'SCULLION. A room? But he may be dangerous. He looks as though he is.

CONNIE. Nonsense! He's just a little tart. Give him a room. Make sure it's a good one. With a double bed. I may be working late tonight.

32. Exterior. A pathway near the house. *A hedge. Beyond the hedge a rose garden. Further off a rose arbour.* McTURK, *travel-stained and woebegone, walks down the pathway. The silvery mists of early morning hang on the distant trees.*
   Suddenly, at the end of the arbour, ROWENA TORRENCE *is seen wearing a filmy négligée.*

33. Exterior. The Rose Arbour. McTURK *is running across the garden and down the arbour to greet* ROWENA. *He calls to her across the silent, dew-drenched garden.*

McTURK. Rowena! Rowena!

34. Exterior. The Rose Arbour. ROWENA TORRENCE *turns to greet* McTURK. *They embrace in the centre of the arbour. He kisses her. Rose petals, each one touched with a pearl of dew, fall slowly upon them.*

ROWENA (*caressing him*). Oh, my darling, what a state you're in. You're muddy and dirty, but I still love you.

McTURK. What are you doing here?

ROWENA. I'm staying here until the convent is ready to receive me. There are one or two minor technicalities like the loss of my virginity which are holding things up.

The arbour swings away from McTURK. The colours dissolve. The shadows reach out to him. He clings to ROWENA.

McTURK. Can you get me something to eat. I'm ready to faint. I've had nothing since yesterday.

ROWENA. You'll have to go to the kitchen. It's much nicer for you there than in the dining-room. I'm sure they'll make you comfy.

She leads him from the arbour. He puts an arm round her waist.

McTURK. I never want to leave you again. We'll be together forever.

ROWENA (*with a tinkly laugh*). Of course we will. Only this morning I'm playing tennis. So you will excuse me, won't you?

She gently pushes his hand away from her waist and smiles.

35. Interior. A large and luxuriously appointed bedroom.
CONNIE *and* LOW *enter.*

CONNIE. I'm just across the hall. If you want me. (*She gives a coarse emphasis to her remarks.*) You've got a shower — (*She pulls back the shower curtain.*) See?

LOW. How much will all this cost?

CONNIE comes close to him. Puts an arm round his waist and squeezes him hard.

CONNIE. Nothing that you can't well afford. (*Seeing his alarm she pinches his cheek.*) A little sweetie, aren't you?

Suddenly he finds her in his arms. They fall onto the bed.

CONNIE. You want someone to look after you. I think I can fit you into my place.

She is unable to restrain herself. She mauls him in a most unexpected manner. His teeth shake. He struggles for breath. A faint yell escapes him before she envelops him completely.

36. Interior. The kitchen of Money-Box Lodge. MISS
DRUMGOOLE *is washing dishes at the sink.* McTURK *is eating
a meal.*

McTURK. What are you doing here? It's a long way to Father
Brodie's pantry.

MISS DRUMGOOLE. I'm accompanying Miss Rowena and
Mrs O'Scullion to the convent. We're only stopping here a
night or two. Naturally I must earn my keep. And so I
opted to help in the kitchen.

She dries her hands. She sits opposite McTURK *and pours
herself a cup of tea.*

MISS DRUMGOOLE (*with a sigh*). I could sit opposite you
forever, Ian McTurk. Has any woman ever said that to you
before?

McTURK. A bus conductress hinted as much once. She gave me
a free ride.

MISS DRUMGOOLE (*with a sentimental smile*). And so would I,
Ian McTurk. If you'd only ask. (*She lifts the cup to her lips.*)
Your mother must've been a lucky woman.

McTURK. No. She was dogged by bad luck. She threw herself
over the balcony of a cinema during a Mario Lanza film.

MISS DRUMGOOLE. And what about your father?

McTURK. He was strangled during a political disturbance.

MISS DRUMGOOLE. Was he demonstrating against the
Government?

McTURK. No. He was selling fruit to passing tourists.

MISS DRUMGOOLE. Life hasn't been kind to you, has it? I'm
afraid it has many more shocks in store for you. Miss Rowena
asked me to see you left the house immediately you'd
finished breakfast.

McTURK *stares.*

McTURK (*pause*). But I love her. She's going to marry me.

MISS DRUMGOOLE *gives a bitter laugh.*

MISS DRUMGOOLE. She's destined for richer hands than
yours.

*She takes him to the window. She lifts the cup with one hand.
Points through the window with the other.*

MISS DRUMGOOLE. That's the man she's going to marry.

37. Exterior. Seen through the kitchen window. ROWENA,
carrying a tennis racket is walking with BERNARD COATES.
They are deep in conversation. MISS DRUMGOOLE's *voice is
heard over the picture.*

MISS DRUMGOOLE. He's made a fortune in the catering trade.
The engagement is to be announced at the Hoteliers' dinner
on Friday.

38. Interior. The kitchen. McTURK *turns to* MISS DRUMGOOLE,
angry.

McTURK. I don't believe you!

MISS DRUMGOOLE. She was afraid that would be your reaction.
She left this letter for you. (*She takes a letter from her
bosom.*) It explains how she fell in love with Bernard Coates
quite suddenly after accidentally seeing his trading figures
for last year.

She gives McTURK *the letter. He opens it. Reads. Tears the
letter to pieces, on the verge of tears.*

McTURK (*pause, bitterly*). I'll never trust a woman again as long
as I live.

He goes to the door.

MISS DRUMGOOLE (*shaking her head*). Another man's heart
Miss Rowena has broken!

39. Interior. A car on a road winding between trees. LOW *is
sitting beside* CONNIE *who is driving. She smiles and squeezes
his leg above the knee. He knocks her hand away, sullen.*

40. Exterior. A country road lined with trees. Early afternoon.
McTURK *walking alone. Rounding a bend in the road he comes
upon a number of* MEN *sitting among the trees. They are*

unshaven and wear old clothes. Two or three tents are pitched nearby. A fire has been lit. McTURK *walks over to them.*

McTURK. Good afternoon. I hope you don't mind my introducing myself to you. My name is Ian McTurk.

A young man who appears to be the leader stands up. He wears a torn army jerkin. His name is JACK RAMSAY.

RAMSAY. My name is John Ramsay. I'm the leader of a semi-political organisation. I call myself Jack and I encourage other people to do the same.

McTURK. I'd like to join your organisation.

RAMSAY. Why?

McTURK. A woman has broken my heart.

RAMSAY. Well, that's as good a reason as any to enter politics. We're planning a series of outrages against society. You're just in time to see the fun. Go and give your name to somebody and report back to me immediately.

41. Exterior. Morning. McTURK **and** RAMSAY **in a large city.** *They pass a hoarding. On it is a picture of Lillian Corbett. The poster says:* 'IF YOU THINK LIKE A WOMAN, VOTE LIKE A WOMAN'.

RAMSAY. We're going to assassinate Mrs Corbett. She's played the fool long enough. I'm putting the finishing touches to my plan. (*He takes a pamphlet from his pocket.*) Read that. It's fresh from the printers.

McTURK. What is it?

RAMSAY. Spicy gossip about people in authority. You see, when we try to undermine people's confidence in the Government of the day we use a variety of tactics: the smear, the lie and, in extreme cases, even the truth.

McTURK *opens the pamphlet.*

42. Close-up of the pamphlet. *It is crudely printed and meant to appeal to the emotions of the lowest level. It shows a flashlight picture of Christopher Low in a bubble bath. A caption says:* 'LATEST ADDITION TO POLICE CHIEF'S HAREM'.

43. Exterior. A public square. *A large crowd of* MEN. RAMSAY *pushes his way to the platform. He mounts the steps. Loud cheers.* RAMSAY *holds up his hands.*

RAMSAY. We all know why we're here! (*The crowd answers with a roar.*) We're here because there's nothing on the telly! Isn't that so?

The crowd answers 'Yes', 'You've never said a truer word', 'Good old Jackie'.

RAMSAY. And what better reason can there be for demonstrating against a Government that has consistently flouted the will of the people!

Several flags are produced and waved. An OLD MAN *next to* McTURK *begins to shout violently.*

OLD MAN. Freedom from tyranny!

McTURK (*with interest*). Are you oppressed?

OLD MAN. No.

McTURK. Then why are you calling for freedom?

OLD MAN. I always do at these meetings. I've been coming to them all my life. (*He waves a flag.*) Death to the oppressors!

RAMSAY (*appealing to the crowd*). I'm one of the fortunate ones. I don't need an excuse to be against the Government. It is in my blood. (*He waves his flag.*) My mum and dad were demonstrating against the import of Japanese goods when I was born. They used my mum's placard as a stretcher. And I'm not ashamed to own it!

The crowd cheers. The OLD MAN *clambers onto the platform.*

OLD MAN. I'm Jackie's dad and I can vouch for every word he says!

RAMSAY *helps the* OLD MAN *up beside him.*

OLD MAN (*addressing the crowd*). I want to speak to you today about the Archbishop of Canterbury. I know, and Jackie here knows (*He smiles and nods to* JACK RAMSAY.) and many of you know, that a month ago she was caught in compromising circumstances. It was hushed up, of course.

Crowd shouts 'Typical!', 'They always get away with it, don't they?' *and* 'What a way for a princess of the Church to behave'. *The* OLD MAN *nods to the crowd.*

OLD MAN. She'd just finished officiating at a ceremony attended by high-ranking ecclesiastics!

He nods and winks. The crowd roars its understanding.

OLD MAN. If you or me had done that sort of thing we'd be in trouble. Owing to her exalted rank the Archbishop got off scot free! (*He turns and speaks off mike to* RAMSAY.) Pass round those scandalous snaps of the Archbishop, Jackie. I've got them going now.

McTURK, RAMSAY *and their helpers hand pamphlets around in the crowd. The* OLD MAN *is heard shouting.*

OLD MAN. This state of affairs is a disgrace! It cannot be allowed to continue! We must fight to the death for our rights!

The crowd cheers. Hats are thrown into the air. Suddenly police whistles are heard. Uniformed POLICEWOMEN *converge onto the square. At the same time* MOUNTED POLICEWOMEN *ride down the panic-stricken crowd.*

McTURK. Is that old man really your father?

RAMSAY. No. But I allow him to think he is.

McTURK. Why?

RAMSAY. There's no time to explain. We must get away from here. Follow me!

They push their way through a chaos of young men and POLICEWOMEN.

44. Exterior. Side streets leading from the square. RAMSAY *and* McTURK *running. Outside a tall, imposing building several* MEN *have chained themselves to the railings.* RAMSAY *gives them an encouraging nod and hurries on.*

RAMSAY (*to* McTURK). These are some of the ways we demonstrate our opposition to the present regime. Later this afternoon my father intends to commit an appalling act in the National Gallery.

45. Interior. The National Gallery. *A painting of a naked Adonis. The* OLD MAN *enters bent nearly double. He takes an axe from* *under his coat and slashes at the picture. Cries of horror from the black* LADY ATTENDANTS *who rush upon him.*

OLD MAN (*struggling in the grip of several* NEGRESSES). I'm making a gesture of defiance! You should be interested in the mind of Man not his body! All you think of is the sensuousness of the male! Look at his mind, you evil beasts!

The ATTENDANTS *carry him away.*

46. Exterior. A street in a sleazy neighbourhood. *A shop-front sign says* 'LULU CODRON — PALMIST'.
    JACK RAMSAY *and* IAN McTURK *arrive at the door, panting.* RAMSAY *knocks. The door is opened an inch or two by the* MAYOR (TERENCE O'SCULLION). *He is poorly dressed, in contrast to the last time* McTURK *saw him. He has a hangdog expression. He opens the door to allow the young men in.* RAMSAY *looks down the street to assure himself that they haven't been followed.*

47. Interior. The back of the shop. Evening. *A dingy, depressing place.* RAMSAY *hands his jerkin and cap to the* MAYOR *and leads the way upstairs.*

McTURK (*dropping back as the* MAYOR *hangs* RAMSAY's *jerkin on a hook*). Aren't you the Lord Mayor of the town where I was born?

MAYOR. I was. My circumstances have been sadly reduced, I'm afraid.

McTURK. Why have you joined this dubious political organisation?

MAYOR. Like most men in positions of trust I was engaged in illegal activities. My own wife denounced me to the authorities. I had to flee to escape a prison sentence. I'm now a wanted man. My only hope of regaining a place in society is by destroying those who brought about my disgrace.

He leads the way upstairs.

48. Interior. The room above the shop. Night. *A large number of* MEN *are gathered together talking, smoking and drinking. The* MAYOR *leads* McTURK *to a table at which* CHRISTOPHER

LOW *is sitting. The table is littered with papers and important-looking documents.*

MAYOR. This is Christopher Low who once blew an arm from the allegorical figure of Peace on the Memorial to the Fallen. I believe you've already met.

McTURK (*to* LOW). Is it true that you're the plaything of the head of the C.I.D?

LOW. Perfectly true. I'm very ashamed of the fact. If only society had treated me better I might not now be plotting to destroy it.

McTURK *sits. The* MAYOR *sits next to him.* RAMSAY *is at the head of the table.* McTURK *is surprised to find* MISS DRUMGOOLE *sitting in the empty space on the other side of him. He gives a shocked exclamation.*

McTURK. Miss Drumgoole! What are you doing here?

MISS DRUMGOOLE. I lost my position as Father Brodie's housekeeper because I'd helped you in your romantic affair with Miss Rowena. I'm now employed as a part-time secretary by the Security Service. My love for you has led me to betray my country. (*A tear falls from her eye.*) I hope that one day you'll be able to repay me.

RAMSAY *leans across.*

RAMSAY (*to* McTURK). Miss Drumgoole is a valuable ally. She's just brought us plans of the Conference which is to be held at the Albert Hall tomorrow.

He gets to his feet. The room falls silent in anticipation. All eyes are upon him.

RAMSAY. Patricia Drumgoole has given up her godless life as housekeeper to a clergyman to join our cause. As far as I know she is the only woman in this room. I shall carry out a thorough check later on.

Everyone looks confident of being able to pass the test.

RAMSAY. Tomorrow, as many of you know, we are going to assassinate the Prime Minister. (*To* CHRISTOPHER LOW.) Make a note of that, will you? I don't want it to slip my mind. (*He turns back to the meeting.*) Our plans have had to be altered slightly. The reason for this being that only women are allowed into the Conference Hall. This problem appeared to be insuperable. Fortunately a solution was quickly found.

49. Exterior. Outside the Conference Hall. *A car draws up.* RAMSAY, McTURK *and* LOW *get out. With heavily made-up eyes, furs and smart hats, they resemble perfectly women of authority and fashion. They enter the Conference Hall.*

50. Interior. The entrance hall. RAMSAY *opens his handbag and shows a card to the uniformed* POLICEWOMAN.

POLICEWOMAN. What's the password?

RAMSAY. 'Irresistible'.

POLICEWOMAN. Would you like to check with Security now?

RAMSAY. Yes.

> *The* POLICEWOMAN *leads the way down a corridor.* RAMSAY, McTURK *and* LOW *follow.*

51. Interior. An office. MISS DRUMGOOLE *is sitting at a typewriter.* CONNIE, *in uniform, sits behind an enormous desk.* CHRISTOPHER LOW *tilts his hat further over, throwing his face into shadow.* RAMSAY *wastes no time. His manner is correct and official.*

RAMSAY (*taking three passes from his handbag*). Here are my passes. I wish to go up immediately.

CONNIE. Where are you from?

RAMSAY. We represent the nice part of Acton.

CONNIE (*to* MISS DRUMGOOLE). See if you've anything under Acton.

> MISS DRUMGOOLE *goes to a filing cabinet.*

RAMSAY. I don't think there's any need for this. We're perfectly respectable girls.

McTURK. My auntie is the spiritual adviser to a baking powder firm.

LOW. And I have connections with several prominent men. There's no need at all to check my bona-fides.

CONNIE (*with a smile*). I'm sorry to cause you inconvenience, but we cannot be too careful. There've been rumours of a plot to kill the P.M.

MISS DRUMGOOLE goes to another filing cabinet, opens it. Leafs through.

CONNIE (*to* RAMSAY). Is this your first Conference?

RAMSAY. Yes.

CONNIE. You needn't be worried. You'll love everybody.

RAMSAY. I was terrified my clothes would be dowdy.

CONNIE. I think you look very smart.

RAMSAY. And my hair — where do you get yours done?
It's so lovely.

CONNIE (*smiles*). I'm so glad you like it. Most people think because a girl's in uniform she doesn't have to worry about her appearance. They couldn't be further from the truth.

Her manner is relaxed. She takes out a hand-mirror and studies her face.

CONNIE. I've been having my hair done at Senora Sally Warren's. She caters almost exclusively for the horse guards, but she may be able to fit you in. (*To* MISS DRUMGOOLE.) Have you got Sally's card?

MISS DRUMGOOLE produces the card from the file. Hands it to RAMSAY.

CONNIE (*with a smile*). Have a bon coiffeur, won't you, dear? (*To* MISS DRUMGOOLE.) I don't think there's any real need to check up. I'm not the suspicious type.

MISS DRUMGOOLE. I'll take these ladies to the Conference Hall, ma'am. Will you be good enough to sign the admittance chit?

CONNIE scribbles her name at the bottom of a half sheet of paper. MISS DRUMGOOLE leads the way into the corridor. CONNIE suddenly focuses her attention on CHRISTOPHER LOW.

CONNIE. I say.

LOW stops.

Have you got a brother? A little brunette. Rather wistful, but quite good fun?

LOW. No.

CONNIE *looks puzzled.* LOW *follows the others.* CONNIE *lights a cigarette.*

52. Interior. The Conference Hall. *Every seat is occupied by a woman. Nurses, nuns, policewomen, uniformed usherettes, representatives of the armed forces. Delegates in their fashionable dresses.* RAMSAY, McTURK *and* LOW *push their way through the throng.*

53. Interior. The Conference Hall. RAMSAY, McTURK *and* LOW. *A group of* WOMEN.

MRS O'SCULLION (*to* RAMSAY). What are you going to wear for the disarmament conference?

RAMSAY. I did think a wool two-piece, simplicity itself, yet with a sort of dash and elegance.

MRS O'SCULLION (*flinging up her hands*). Oh, how perfect!

LOW. I think it would be fun if our delegates wore matching costumes.

MRS O'SCULLION. What a perfectly marvellous idea! (*She turns to the woman beside her.*) We must tell Lillian about this wonderful idea!

54. Interior. The Conference Hall. *A flurry as the* PRIME MINISTER *arrives. She is beautifully dressed.*
A burst of applause. Several hundred WOMEN *sway with excitement.*
The PRIME MINISTER *takes her place at a table on the platform. Flashlight photographs are taken.*

55. Interior. A box overlooking the conference platform. RAMSAY, McTURK *and* LOW *open their handbags. In each is a section of a telescopic rifle.* RAMSAY *assembles the rifle.*

56. Interior. The Conference Hall. The platform. *The* PRIME MINISTER *addresses herself to the microphones in front of her.*

PRIME MINISTER. This is my first report as Prime Minister and I'd like to commence by paying to the ladies of the cabinet an immediate tribute. How they manage to run the country and remain so attractive I do not know.

She turns off the mike and speaks to a middle-aged woman.

PRIME MINISTER. I think you're looking simply splendid after your facial, Pixie.

The WOMAN *smiles modestly.*
The PRIME MINISTER *turns back to the microphones.*

PRIME MINISTER. Well, dears, we've just had the most heavenly cabinet meeting!

MRS O'SCULLION *struggles to her feet. Her face is flushed. Her lip trembles.*

MRS O'SCULLION. Oh, Lillian! And I wasn't there! How could you!

PRIME MINISTER. The very next time, darling. (*With a consolatory smile.*)

MRS O'SCULLION. No! You've betrayed my trust. I wouldn't come now if you begged me!

She stamps her foot. Bursts into tears. Dabbing her eyes she runs from the platform. The PRIME MINISTER *sighs.*

PRIME MINISTER. Georgina gets so excited by the smallest things. I sometimes wonder whether it was altogether wise to give her the Foreign Office. (*She flicks ash from her cigarette end.*) We had the meeting at Molly's house. And we've come to a decision that is sure to have far-reaching consequences.

A flutter of anticipation.

PRIME MINISTER. We're having the House of Commons redecorated in Chinese white lacquer and natural oak woodwork!

Every woman in the hall gives an exclamation of delight. A shimmer of silk, a sway of feathers, the tinkling of ten thousand pearls.

57. Interior. The box. RAMSAY *has assembled the rifle.*
LOW *and* McTURK *open their handbags. They take out lipsticks.*

They turn up the lipsticks. In each is a bullet. They hand the bullets to RAMSAY *who loads the rifle.*

58. Interior. The Conference Hall. The platform. *The* PRIME MINISTER *has just been given a standing ovation. She consults her notes.*

PRIME MINISTER. And now, the International field — this afternoon I shall put a stop to speculation. I shall attend the disarmament conference in a great flowing dress in white broderie Anglaise with heavenly flounces. The price was simply outrageous!

59. Interior. The box. *The door is abruptly pushed open.* RAMSAY, *holding the rifle, is pressed back against the wall.* CONNIE *looks in.*

CONNIE (*in a whisper*). We're having trouble downstairs with a group who say they're from Acton. Could you come and help us sort it out?

McTURK. We must stay and hear the end of the Prime Minister's speech.

CONNIE *smiles, looks down onto the platform. The* PRIME MINISTER *is smiling.*

CONNIE. She has the most perfect set of teeth I've ever seen.

LOW. And all her own. So they say.

McTURK. Is it true that she's the brains behind a chain of beauty salons?

CONNIE. Yes.

LOW. They haven't done much for her, have they?

CONNIE *giggles.*

CONNIE. Now then, we mustn't talk like that. (*With a wink.*) Though I couldn't agree with you more. She is hideous! (*Swings heavily on the door of the box.*) See you in a jiffy then?

She closes the door and leaves the box laughing. RAMSAY *steps from behind the door and takes aim at the platform.*

60. Interior. The Conference Hall. The platform. *A* WOMAN
REPORTER *is questioning the* PRIME MINISTER.

REPORTER. Will there be an official statement, Prime Minister?

PRIME MINISTER. Yes. Doors are closed to further negotiations.
My wardrobe is complete.

REPORTER. Lillian, if you are asked to take part in a four-girl
meeting in the Autumn will you go?

PRIME MINISTER. Well, it depends on the aims and terms of such
a meeting. I'm in favour of direct contact with our rivals, as
you know, but after the disgraceful things they said about my
drawing-room curtains last time, I don't think I can make too
great an effort to be polite.

*She looks around the hall with a hurt expression. The entire
conference is with her on this point.*

61. Interior. The box. RAMSAY *takes aim at the distant figure of
the* PRIME MINISTER. McTURK *and* LOW *drop back. A burst
of applause.* RAMSAY *pulls the trigger. A shot is heard. He puts
the rifle down. They all let themselves out of the box and enter
the corridor.*

62. Interior. The Conference Hall. *Women are fainting, row by
row, falling to the ground in hysterics. On the platform a number
of delegates have passed out. They have dropped from their chairs
and are awaiting medical treatment. The dead body of the* PRIME
MINISTER *is being removed by the ambulance staff.* POLICE-
WOMEN *hurry to and fro questioning witnesses.* TRAINED
NURSES *attempt to give medical attention. As quickly as one
woman is revived another faints.*

63. Interior. A staircase. RAMSAY, McTURK *and* LOW *hurry
down.* CONNIE *appears at the bottom of the stairs with a tall
woman. The three young men stop. They continue their descent
in a more orderly manner.* CONNIE *meets them. Her manner is
frigid.*

CONNIE. This is Tess Eliot. She runs a dyeworks in the
Bridgenorth Road. She claims to represent Acton.

TESS ELIOT. I was elected by my fellow workers in Bijou garments. Do you mind telling me just what you're playing at?

The door behind them bursts open and MRS O'SCULLION *rushes in.*

MRS O'SCULLION (*waving her arms, hysterically*). Lilly's been done in! We shall all have to go into mourning!

CONNIE *turns to the young men, her suspicions confirmed. Before she can speak* RAMSAY *brings her low with a flying tackle.* McTURK *hits* TESS ELIOT *with his handbag.* LOW *shoves* MRS O'SCULLION *to one side. Hundreds of screaming women are suddenly upon them, flooding from the conference hall. The boys run down the corridor.* CONNIE *sits up, dazed, crying aloud in surprise.*

CONNIE. They were men!

64. Exterior. A street. *The boys running.* RAMSAY *stops at a news-stand to buy a paper. He opens it.*

65. Page of print. *Three 'Identikit' pictures. Headline:* 'Have you seen these men?'

66. Exterior. Another street. *The boys enter, running. Out of breath. They stop near a newsagents. They go inside.*

67. Interior. The newsagent's shop. RAMSAY's *father is behind the counter. He looks up when the three young men enter.*

RAMSAY'S FATHER. You've struck a blow for freedom, Jackie. Your mother's face went white when she heard what you'd done. I was being forcibly fed by her. She cursed you. She said you were the type of son no mother should love. I threw my gruel at her. I've always found her a most disgusting woman, as you may have heard me say.

RAMSAY. When did you get out of prison?

RAMSAY'S FATHER. Not two hours ago. I was released on the personal say-so of the Governor of Brixton. Your mother, as a common or garden wardress, had no option but to release me.

He pulls a copy of a newspaper from a rack behind him and shoves it under RAMSAY's *face.*

RAMSAY'S FATHER. Look at that, Jackie. Lady Cudlipp has done you proud!

68. Newspaper Headline: 'A Nation Mourns!'

69. Exterior. A broad thoroughfare leading to a cathedral. *With official pomp, increased by security arrangements, the coffin containing the body of the late* PRIME MINISTER, *is carried on a gun carriage to its last resting place. Slow March.*
   Mourning figures led by the ARCHBISHOP OF CANTERBURY, DR MAUD ELPHINSTONE. *Flags are much in evidence.*
RAMSAY, McTURK *and* LOW *with a number of revolutionaries appear at the head of the procession. They bar the way into the cathedral.*
   The ARCHBISHOP OF CANTERBURY *raises her hands in saintly horror.*

ARCHBISHOP. I'm a Princess of the Church! Let me pass. I've some hard praying to do.

   RAMSAY *thrusts her aside. Cries of* 'Sacrilege' *and* 'Blasphemy' *mingled with* 'The last days are come' *from the multitude.*

RAMSAY (*addressing the crowd*). Who are your leaders? What do you know of their private lives?

   The crowd are uneasy.

RAMSAY. I'm going to speak plainly. Pardon me if I give offence. Facts are often unpleasant. I was privileged recently to attend a select dinner in the home of a high-ranking member of the Government. During the meal she behaved in a way which left me in no doubt as to her intentions. Afterwards she suggested that I accompany her on a trip to ratify an international treaty. All expenses paid. I refused, knowing that what she proposed was wrong. How many other lads has she tried to intimidate in this vile way.

LOW. I was the passing fancy of the head of the C.I.D.

   RAMSAY'S FATHER *is seen on the edge of the crowd.*

RAMSAY'S FATHER. She ruined his life. I've often heard him say so. Her kisses set his blood on fire!

LOW. Let's overthrow the Government. That is the solution to all our problems.

RAMSAY. We'll pass a law forbidding anyone to entertain in private. We cannot afford this stifling secrecy.

McTURK. Anything that is worth doing is worth doing in public.

Cheers. RAMSAY'S FATHER *waves his handkerchief.*

RAMSAY'S FATHER. Death to the oppressors! Liberty! Down with the tyrants!

Wild cheering. Fighting breaks out round the gun carriage. The ARCHBISHOP OF CANTERBURY *and her fellow clerics drop to their knees in prayer.*

70. Exterior. The area round the cathedral. *Police appear and make baton charges. Shots are exchanged between* POLICE-WOMEN *and* RIOTERS. *The crowd scatters in panic. The rebels fight it out with the police across the gun carriage and heads of the kneeling clerics. The representatives of the legal government cower behind the pillars of the cathedral.*
Across the picture appears a ticker-tape message which reads: 'Anarchy rumours strong denial from Whitehall'.

71. Exterior. Several streets around the cathedral. *Pitched battles between* POLICE *and* RIOTERS. RAMSAY *and his men round up a number of pro-government supporters — mostly blondes.* POLICEWOMEN *fire on rebel troop positions. Scenes of wild disorder.*
Across the picture appears a ticker-tape message which reads: 'Strong woman needed says "Pixie" Heath'.

72. Exterior. Street. Mid-day. RAMSAY'S FATHER *is seen selling newspapers.*

RAMSAY'S FATHER (*calling hoarsely*). 'Police chief elected President!'

He holds up a newspaper.

73. Headline from the newspaper: 'Gorgeous Connie in Downing Street'.

74. Interior. The cabinet room in Downing Street. CONNIE *is seated with a number of prominent ministers.* ROWENA *is ushered into the room.* CONNIE *rises, smiling.*

CONNIE. Ah, my dear, come in. Did you have a pleasant honeymoon?

ROWENA. Yes. My husband was nearly killed.

CONNIE. Good. Everything is going according to plan then. Take a seat.

ROWENA *sits.*

CONNIE. You know the rest of the girls, don't you? (*The other women smile.*) As you've probably heard, dear, we've had a spot of bother since Lilly died. Everything north of the Humber is in male hands. Even Girl Guides and Brownies have tales to tell that make hardened matrons blush. We must do something. And quickly.

ROWENA. How can I help?

CONNIE. We've discovered the identity of one of the rebel leaders. His name is Ian McTurk.

ROWENA. Oh, I know him. I was going to marry him once. He was sent away from the town where he was born for my sake.

CONNIE (*with a smile*). I'd like you to use your influence for the public good. Once we have their leaders the rebellion can quickly be crushed.

She smiles around the table. The other women nod in agreement.

75. Interior. The shop. *The windows are crowded with men firing into the street.* RAMSAY *hurries up to* McTURK. *He hands him a note.*

RAMSAY. This note has just been delivered. It's addressed to you in a woman's hand.

McTURK *opens the letter. His eyes swim with tears. He reads:*

76. The letter. *It says:* 'My darling. Please forgive me for what I did. I must see you to explain. Yours ever — Rowena Coates.'

77. Interior. The shop. McTURK *folds up the letter.*

McTURK. It's from Rowena. She still loves me.

RAMSAY. It may be a trap.

McTURK. She asks for my forgiveness. I must go to her.

He hands his rifle to RAMSAY *and hurries away.* RAMSAY *takes his place in the firing line.*

78. Exterior. The garden of a town house. *High walls and long unweeded flowerbeds. Moonlight.* McTURK *advances. At the end of the garden he sees* ROWENA. *He runs to her across the dew-laden grass. He kisses her. Buries his head on her breast.*

McTURK. I love you so. Don't ever leave me again.

Her arms are about him.

ROWENA. Oh, my poor darling, how unhappy I've made you.

She kisses him. As she does so a number of uniformed POLICEWOMEN *surround them. They drag* McTURK *away. Without looking at him* ROWENA *turns and leaves the garden. She meets* CONNIE.

CONNIE (*patting her shoulder*). You did very well. We're all proud of you.

79. Exterior. The shop. *The signal for a final assault is given. The shop is attacked on all sides by screaming women waving rifles. They batter down the door and shoot at the rebels inside.*

80. Exterior. The roof of the shop. RAMSAY *climbs across the tiles with a flag. He sticks the flag on the highest point of the roof.*

RAMSAY. Long live the glorious revolution!

A fusilade of bullets is fired from the POLICEWOMEN *below.* RAMSAY *staggers across the roof back to the skylight. He clutches his heart. He falls fainting.* CHRISTOPHER LOW *climbs from the skylight and crawls across the roof to* RAMSAY. RAMSAY *has raised himself a little. Blood pours from his wounds.* LOW *helps him up. As they reach the skylight another round of shots is fired from the police.* RAMSAY *and* LOW *sway together. Another round. Cries of horror from below as* RAMSAY *slumps forward and crashes over the edge of the roof onto the pavement taking* LOW *with him.*

81. Exterior. The shop. CONNIE *and her detectives are seen handcuffing lines of men and leading them into waiting buses.* McTURK *is put into a police van and driven away.*

82. Exterior. A wharf. Night. McTURK *is led from the car and down a flight of steps to a waiting motor launch. The launch heads for the open sea.*

83. Exterior. A landing stage. *The launch is tied up. One of the guards leaps ashore.* McTURK *is dragged up the steps. A* GUARD *follows with a rifle.*

84. Interior. A prison cell. *The door is opened and* McTURK *is shoved inside by the* GUARD.

GUARD. Here's your kip for tonight. It's late and the Governor is asleep. He might change you tomorrow.

McTURK *looks around him. The door is banged shut. He hammers on the door.*

McTURK. I haven't had a trial!

GUARD. If you're guilty a trial is a waste of public money.

McTURK. Everybody must have a trial. That's the rules.

GUARD. The rules have been changed.

McTURK. Are they allowed to do that?

GUARD. It makes no difference to you whether they're allowed to change the rules or not. (*Pause.*) You can have less food. That's allowed.

McTURK. What else is allowed?

GUARD. Books. And the occasional woman — if you care for that type of thing.

McTURK. I want to see the Governor.

GUARD. He's asleep. Make an application in the morning.

He switches out the light. McTURK *sits on his bunk. He buries his head in his hands.*

85. Interior. The Governor's room. *The* GOVERNOR (BERNARD COATES) *is seated at a table, a file before him.* McTURK *is led into the room by the* GUARD. BERNARD COATES *takes* McTURK's *hand.*

BERNARD COATES. How are you, my boy? We met once before I believe, under happier circumstances.

He shakes his head. Sits at the desk. Opens the file.

What made you decide to overthrow the Government of the country? Was it a childhood ambition?

McTURK. It would take too long to explain.

BERNARD COATES. You've been given a twenty year sentence. Isn't that time enough?

McTURK. Surely I've the right to appeal?

BERNARD COATES. Under normal circumstances a prisoner does have the right of appeal. However, in your case, the authorities have decided to waive that right.

McTURK. Why?

BERNARD COATES. I couldn't say. Would you like me to find out?

McTURK. Yes.

BERNARD COATES (*turns to the* GUARD). Why has the right of appeal been withheld from the prisoner?

GUARD (*salutes smartly*). The prisoner has been denied the right of appeal on grounds of height, sir!

BERNARD COATES (*turns back to* McTURK *with a sympathetic shake of the head*). You're too small to lodge an appeal McTurk. There's nothing I can do for you, I'm afraid. Is there anything you'd like to alleviate your condition?

McTURK. I'd like a better cell. The one I have at the moment is filthy.

BERNARD COATES. Well, that's simple enough. (*To the* GUARD.) See the prisoner is put into a better cell. (*To* McTURK.) Come and see me any time. I'm always ready to help you.

McTURK and the GUARD *leave the room.*

86. Interior. Another cell. *The door is opened.* McTURK *is shoved inside.* McTURK *stares about him in horror. It is worse than the first. There is no bunk. The walls are peeling. A film of grime covers everything. There is a heap of straw in the corner. The* GUARD *bangs the door.* McTURK *shouts through the door.*

McTURK. I want to see the Governor. He promised to see my quarters were better. These are much worse.

GUARD (*looking through the spy-hole*). I wish you wouldn't complain. It only makes things worse.

The sound of his feet retreating along the corridor is heard. McTURK *sits upon the floor. He buries his face in his hands in despair.*

87. Interior. The cell. *On the wall of the cell is a calendar. On the calendar is a young girl in the briefest of bikinis. She is posed with a beach ball. Leaves are torn from the calendar as the days pass. Snow falls outside the window.* McTURK, *unshaven, ragged, wild, with straws in his hair, accepts food from the* GUARD. *He eats the food on the floor. The door bangs shut.*
Green leaves show outside the window. The girl on the calendar grows older. From being a lovely seventeen-year-old she matures into a ripe twenty-seven. More leaves are torn from the calendar. It is raining outside, McTURK *lies in the straw in the corner of the cell. Half-naked, hairy, bestial. The* GUARD *opens the door, pushes the food inside, shuts the door with a bang. Ice has formed around the windows. Icicles hang from the walls. The woman on the calendar is a matron of thirty-seven. The cell grows dark.*
McTURK sleeps, half buried in the straw. The woman on the calendar is old, grey-haired, withered. She still holds up the beach ball with a gay smile. She has no teeth. Her smile is hideous.
The sun shines into the window. It is summer. McTURK *scratches himself. A noise is heard. A tapping and scraping.* McTURK *sits up and listens. The next instant a part of the floor gives way and he topples into a deep hole which appears under him. Finding no bones broken he stands to his feet.*

88. Interior. A roughly-hewn tunnel. *In the semi-darkness* JACK RAMSAY *leans on a shovel.*

RAMSAY. Hallo. I've come to rescue you.

McTURK. But I've been in prison for ten years. What kept you so long?

RAMSAY. I had several things to attend to. I came as quickly as I could.

McTURK. I thought you'd been killed when you fell off the roof.

RAMSAY. No. I've a strong constitution. I gave up being a revolutionary and married a woman in the diplomatic service. I've lived abroad for many years. My wife recently divorced me.

McTURK. For what reason?

RAMSAY. She found a letter from a strange woman in my wallet. I'd rather not go into details just now. I packed my bags and went back to my father. He persuaded me to join forces with his revolutionary front. My mother and he were at loggerheads again. It's quite impossible living at home these days. And so we raised a small rebellion up north somewhere. It's progressing nicely I believe.

McTURK. What happened to Christopher Low who was my best friend?

RAMSAY. He broke his neck.

McTURK. He's dead?

RAMSAY. No. He's having a wild affair with the Matron of a hospital. His temperature has never been below a hundred in ten years.

McTURK *moves along the tunnel examining RAMSAY's work.*

McTURK. Where does this tunnel lead?

RAMSAY. I don't know.

McTURK *moves back along the tunnel. He picks up the shovel.*

McTURK. If we dig a little further we can break into the main sewer and escape that way.

He begins to dig.

89. Interior. The cell. Evening. *The* GUARD *opens the door. Brings in a bowl of soup. Puts it on the floor. Looks around for* *the prisoner. Kicks at the straw. Sees the hole. Scratches his head. Looks down into the hole. Puzzled.*

GUARD (*calling*). What are you doing down there?

90. Interior. The tunnel. McTURK *and* RAMSAY *are digging. A large hole is made in the wall. They climb through into a sewer.*

91. Interior. The sewer. McTURK *and* RAMSAY *advance cautiously. After a while they reach a point where the tunnel divides into two. They stop. Stare. Lights are seen behind them. Moving guards. Sound of voices.*

McTURK. We're being followed!

92. Interior. Another part of the tunnel. *The* GUARD *leads a number of men. They are following* McTURK *and* RAMSAY.

GUARD. Shoot anything that moves. That's an order.

He moves. They shoot him. He collapses into the sewer and is carried away by the swiftly flowing waters.

93. Interior. The sewer. McTURK *and* RAMSAY *stumble forward to an iron-ribbed grating. The water disappears under the grating. There is no way of escape.*

McTURK. We've got to swim for it!

He kicks off his boots and wades into the water. He ducks under the grating and disappears. RAMSAY *does the same.*

94. Exterior. The open sea. Day. McTURK *and* RAMSAY *are swimming. Waves slide past, white and green, ridge upon ridge, disappearing into drifts where the horizon erases the ridges. A yacht is seen in the distance driven on by the force of the wind. The two men wave, cry out.*

95. Exterior. The side of the yacht. *The boys swim up. A rope is lowered. They are helped out of the water by deckhands.*

96. Exterior. The deck of the yacht.

McTURK (*to a deckhand*). Take us to your Captain.

The deckhand leads the way below.

97. Interior. The yacht. *The two men stand outside a door marked* 'Captain'. *They knock. A voice calls* 'Come in'. *They enter the cabin.*

98. Interior. The Captain's cabin. *The two men enter and are surprised to see* CHRISTOPHER LOW, *in a white uniform, standing at the desk.*

McTURK (*open-mouthed*). Are you the Captain?

LOW. No. I'm the cabin boy.

McTURK. What are you doing here?

LOW. Well, after I recovered from my wounds I was kept a prisoner by the Matron of the Hospital. She insisted that I was not well enough to travel. Tiring of this kind of life I rebelled at last and thumbed a lift on an ambulance that was going to the scene of a fatal accident. On the way there the ambulance was stopped at a road-block. Fearing discovery I ran into a nearby wood. In the middle of the wood I met a rich woman who was picnicking in the nude.

RAMSAY. Why was she doing a thing like that?

LOW. She said she was the most modern woman in the world and she invited me to join her in her 'with it' mode of life. (*To McTURK.*) Her name is Rowena Coates née Torrence.

McTURK appears about to swoon.

McTURK. I gave my heart to her and she betrayed me. I can't stay here.

RAMSAY. We can't leave. We're forty miles west of Ireland.

LOW. You can't stay. Rowena is married to Bernard Coates. He's the Governor of the prison from which you've just escaped.

The door opens and ROWENA *enters. She gives a gasp of surprise upon seeing McTURK.*

McTURK. I suppose you'll turn me over to the police.

ROWENA (*gives a tinkly laugh*). Of course not. Nobody does that kind of thing nowadays. Come and meet my husband. He'll be so pleased to hear you've escaped.

McTURK. I'd like to wash and change my clothes. I've been sleeping in them for years.

ROWENA. What a virile attitude you have to life! Would you like a shower?

McTURK. Yes.

ROWENA. Come with me then. I'll take a shower with you.

RAMSAY *looks shocked.*

RAMSAY. We can't take a shower with you. You're a woman.

ROWENA. Would you like to take one with my husband? I'll call him. He'll be delighted to oblige.

She turns and exits. She can be heard calling.

ROWENA (*outside the cabin*). Bernie! Bernie! One of your prisoners has escaped! Do come and take a shower with him!

99. Interior. The Captain's cabin. *A dinner party is in progress.* ROWENA, BERNARD COATES, *the* MAYOR *and* MRS O'SCULLION, MISS DRUMGOOLE *and a number of other guests including the fat man that* CHRISTOPHER LOW *once rescued from the hole in the forest.* BERNARD COATES *turns to* McTURK. *He puts a hand on his knee in a friendly way.*

BERNARD COATES (*with a smile*). My wife, as I expect you've already been told, is the most modern woman in the world. I'd be a real old stick-in-the-mud without her.

He laughs to himself and spoons soup from his plate.

McTURK. This soup tastes modern enough. What's it made of?

BERNARD COATES. I never ask. Our cabin boy brings us anything he fancies. He escaped from a mental home, you know?

CHRISTOPHER LOW *leans over* McTURK. *Pours soup into his plate.*

LOW. I was strapped down for a week. I thought my mind was going to give way.

ROWENA (*with a tinkly laugh*). And it did finally, didn't it? (*She turns to* MRS O'SCULLION.) He went off his head with the strain of being declared insane!

MRS O'SCULLION. Fascinating. You always meet such interesting people, Rowena.

BERNARD COATES (*to* McTURK). Rowena came home one day with this young man. I've been insulted in the woods, she said. (*He laughs and drinks a little wine.*) I suppose he'd raped her or something. What would we do without the contemporary scene!

ROWENA *looks round the table with a bright, wholesome expression.*

ROWENA. I was being 'nudies' on our country estate when this perfectly mad creature rushes upon me. He'd just crashed the ambulance which was taking him to a place of stricter confinement. I just had to offer him a job.

CHRISTOPHER LOW *splashes soup down her dress. She rises to her feet with a scream.* LOW *shuffles away.*

ROWENA (*with a fluttery laugh*). Don't worry. He's not in control of himself, you see. I'll just go and change my gown.

She hurries away. The MAYOR *leans across to* McTURK.

MAYOR. I'm the Mayor of the town where you were born. I remember your disgrace well.

McTURK. Weren't you involved in the plot to assassinate the Prime Minister?

MAYOR. How nice of you to remember.

McTURK. What are you doing here? I thought you were a wanted man.

MAYOR. My wife withdrew the charges she had made against me and I returned to normal life. I made a fortune in dishonest dealings on the Stock Exchange. I met Bernie through a mutual friend who was the idol of the bistros. He'd just sawn a woman in half.

McTURK. Any conjuror can do that.

MAYOR. Ah, but my friend wasn't a conjuror. He was a

plumber's mate. The girl was expecting his child. It was most distressing. The only solution was a number 2 saw and a trip to the left luggage office at Victoria Station.

He dabs his mouth with a napkin. MISS DRUMGOOLE *leans across to* McTURK *with a shy smile.*

MISS DRUMGOOLE. You probably don't remember me, Ian McTurk. I'm the revolutionary Patricia Drumgoole. A graduate of Father Brodie's pantry.

McTURK. How did you come to be on this yacht with a class of person you once affected to despise?

MISS DRUMGOOLE. I was sharing a room in a girls' hostel with a young socialite who was invited to this yachting party. She was too bored to accept the invitation and suggested that I go in her place.

McTURK. Are you enjoying yourself?

MISS DRUMGOOLE. No. I'd rather be married to you.

McTURK. That's impossible. My heart is broken.

CHRISTOPHER LOW *has cleared the soup plates from the table. As he is halfway across the cabin he drops them. The whole table looks up sharply and then pretends not to have noticed.* RAMSAY *hurries over and helps* LOW *pick up the broken dishes.*

RAMSAY (*in an angry whisper*). What's the matter with you? Are you on the pill again?

LOW. These people expect a mental patient to behave like a mental patient.

RAMSAY. You're not a mental patient.

LOW. They don't know that. I'm a great success as a lunatic.

They put the tray aside. LOW *opens a serving hatch. Food is passed through to him.*

RAMSAY. What was in the soup? It was disgusting.

LOW. It was tinned mushrooms. And I boiled a packet of cigars with it.

RAMSAY. I find this unashamed luxury pointless and soul destroying.

He goes back to his place at the table.

100. Exterior. The deck of the yacht. Moonlight. *The sails billow in a light breeze. Only the sound of the ocean disturbs the tranquil calm of the night.* McTURK *strolls with* ROWENA. *They stop beside a lifebelt fixed to the rail. Painted on the belt is the name of the yacht,* 'The Fairy Wish'.

McTURK. You're more beautiful than ever in the moonlight. The years have made no difference to my feelings for you. I'd like to take you in my arms and kiss you.

He moves closer. She smiles and steps away.

ROWENA. Tell me about your adventures since we last met.

McTURK. I've had no adventures. I haven't seen a woman for ten years. (*Pause.*) I can see through that dress.

ROWENA. After ten years in the company of men that in itself is an adventure.

He takes her hand. Presses her fingers to his lips.

McTURK. If you only knew how, through the long, lonely nights in my prison cell, I've yearned for the touch of your hand.

She smiles. He kisses her lips.

McTURK. Why did you marry Bernard? Was it because he's rich?

ROWENA. Yes.

McTURK. How tragic that I had to be born poor.

He folds her in his arms. The MAYOR *approaches smoking a cigar. They break from their embrace.*

MAYOR. Bernie sent me up to look for you. We're going to look at the stars through my wife's telescope. It should be fun. Won't you join us?

ROWENA *pulls her wrap about her shoulders and goes below. The* MAYOR *smiles. He raises his eyebrows in a cynical way.*

MAYOR. Be careful what you're doing. Bernie is a very jealous man.

McTURK (*haughtily*). When I want your advice I'll ask for it!

He goes below. A disagreeable expression passes over the MAYOR's *face.*

101. Interior. The lounge of the yacht. Morning. McTURK, RAMSAY *and* LOW. LOW *serves coffee from a tray.*

LOW (*handing coffee to* RAMSAY). Miss Drumgoole was washed overboard last night. She left a tin of biscuits in her cabin. Do either of you want them?

RAMSAY. How did it happen?

LOW. She was crossing the desk in the dark when she mistook the handrail for the companionway. The watch heard a cry of 'woman overboard' but thought it was a joke.

McTURK. I refused her hand in marriage last night. I had to be brutal with her. This persistent importuning is most embarrassing.

RAMSAY. She took her life from disappointment. You mustn't feel guilty. You did all you could.

McTURK. I've no intention of feeling guilty. I leave that to Liberal politicians and clergymen. They get paid for it.

He fits a cigarette into a long holder.

McTURK. Rowena has consented to meet me in her cabin at noon. I'm going to give her a good raping. You won't either of you disturb me, will you?

He drinks coffee. RAMSAY *and* CHRISTOPHER LOW *look on in disapproval.*

102. Interior. ROWENA's cabin. *A large daybed with cushions.* ROWENA *paces the cabin. She touches her hair with a nervous gesture. A knock at the door. She calls out in a gay voice to conceal her apprehension.*

ROWENA. Come in!

McTURK *enters.*

McTURK (*closing the door behind him*). They're holding a 'silent ten minutes' in memory of the woman who was washed overboard last night. We shan't be interrupted.

He seizes her in his arms. She gives a little squeak of fright.

ROWENA. We shouldn't be doing this. Think of my husband.
McTURK. I wish you wouldn't keep harping on your husband. I took a shower with him yesterday. What more do you want?

He kisses her on the mouth. They fall among the cushions. She struggles. Pushes him away.

ROWENA. No! Please go away! (*She bursts into tears.*) I shall ring for the steward.

McTURK. What d'you want the steward for when I'm here?

He takes off his shirt. ROWENA *gives a cry of horror.*

ROWENA. What are those scars on your back? Are they the marks of the lash?

McTURK. No. I've been wearing an overtight string vest. (*Puts an arm round her.*) How would you like me? I do a very nice semi-nude.

ROWENA *stands to her feet. Her face is flushed.*

ROWENA. You must go. I can't allow you to behave in this terrible way. It's wrong and we should be ashamed of ourselves.

McTURK *stares at her. Puzzled.*

McTURK. I thought you were the most modern woman in the world.

ROWENA (*with a toss of her hair*). What's that got to do with it?

McTURK. Well, I thought modern birds lived for this kind of thing.

ROWENA (*gives a cold smile. Goes to the door*). I'm afraid you're quite wrong. Being modern has nothing to do with playing nasties. Will you kindly leave my cabin or I shall inform my husband of your disgraceful conduct.

McTURK *picks up his shirt and, shame-faced, leaves the cabin.*

103. Exterior. The deck of the yacht. *The guests are gathered in a circle. Many of them have black ribbons round their arms. They sing the hymn* 'Now the labourer's task is o'er'. *They bow their heads at the end of the hymn.*

MRS O'SCULLION. I've known Patty Drumgoole for years. She was a really kind, sweet girl.

MAYOR. She was rather a plain girl, I thought.

MRS O'SCULLION. She was our parlour maid, don't you remember? I lent her to Father Brodie who never returned her.

RAMSAY. The world will be a sadder place now she's gone.

The crowd stand silent. Many are weeping. The fat man who CHRISTOPHER LOW *once rescued from the hole in the forest passes by.*

FAT MAN (*calling gaily*). The sandpit is open!

The guests begin to drift away. RAMSAY *seizes the* FAT MAN *by the arm, shakes him roughly.*

RAMSAY. A woman was drowned last night! Doesn't that mean anything to you?

The FAT MAN *says nothing. Suddenly he punches* RAMSAY *in the mouth.* RAMSAY *reels away, his mouth and nose bleeding. The* FAT MAN *hurries after the others.* RAMSAY *sinks into a deckchair, mops his mouth and nose with a handkerchief.* CHRISTOPHER LOW *appears with a tray of iced drinks.*

LOW. I once rescued that man from a hole in a forest. He was a prisoner.

McTURK. How did he reward you?

LOW. He knocked two of my teeth out.

He puts a glass down beside RAMSAY.

RAMSAY. I've just remonstrated with him over his callous behaviour in the face of human misery.

LOW. What did he do?

RAMSAY (*spitting blood into his handkerchief*). He knocked two of my teeth out.

McTURK *sits down beside them. He has an expression of complete despair on his face.*

McTURK. We're going to be asked to leave the boat. I've just had an argument with Bernie.

RAMSAY. What about?

McTURK. His wife. He saw me leaving her cabin and became suspicious. I believe he's insanely jealous.

BERNARD COATES *stands in front of them. With him is the* FAT MAN. *The rest of the guests are behind him, watching.*

BERNARD COATES (*to* RAMSAY). Why did you insult the President of the Humpty-Dumpty club?

RAMSAY. I didn't.

FAT MAN (*to* BERNARD). I was on my way to the sandpit
when this hooligan grabbed me by the arm and hurled abuse
at me.

Everyone waits for RAMSAY's *explanation.*

RAMSAY. I wanted him to face up to the realities of human existence.

BERNARD COATES *gives an impatient sniff.*

BERNARD COATES. As I think I told you last night, my outlook
is broadminded, go-ahead and thoroughly up-to-date, but I
won't have people insulting my guests or making free with
my wife. There's a gunboat in the immediate vicinity of this
ship. I've been in radio contact. You'll be taken off my hands
and sent to prison.

*He turns on his heel and strides away. The guests follow,
applauding him for the strong measures he has taken.*
RAMSAY, McTURK *and* LOW *sit in gloom.*

LOW (*standing to his feet at last*). I shall take the lifeboat and
escape. Does anyone care to join me?

He walks away along the deck. The others hesitate and follow.

104. Exterior. The open sea. *A storm. The lifeboat sinks lower
in the water, is tossed about by the fury of the waves. The*
YOUNG MEN *attempt to row. Lose the oars. Drift helplessly. In
the middle of the watery chaos a spar is seen floating towards
them. A* WOMAN *is clinging to it.* CHRISTOPHER LOW *stands
to his feet. The others pull him back.*

LOW. Look! It's Miss Drumgoole!

*The boat rocks. Water pours in over the sides. The spar drifts
nearer.*

McTURK. There's no room for any more. You'll sink the boat!

RAMSAY. We can't leave her to drown. That'd be a monstrous
thing to do.

LOW *and* RAMSAY *fling out a rope to* MISS DRUMGOOLE
who clings to it. The storm rages. They drag her aboard.

MISS DRUMGOOLE. Oh, thank goodness, you saw me. I thought
my last hour had come.

LOW. We couldn't leave a fellow human being to die. We had to rescue you.

The wind howls and the boat sinks beneath the added weight. They all four are thrown into the water. At the mercy of the elements and on the point of death they all cry for help. The wind howls louder and no one answers.

105. Exterior. A beach. McTURK *drags himself from the sea, exhausted, his clothes torn to shreds. A party of* YOUNG NURSES *are playing on the sands. A tall, imperious* WOMAN *is with them.* McTURK *approaches. One of the* NURSES *screams.* McTURK *stumbles forward and faints.*

106. Interior. A hospital ward. McTURK *is in bed. He stares about him, bringing the room into focus. At the end of the bed is the tall, imperious* WOMAN *in the uniform of a hospital* MATRON. *With her is* CONNIE.

McTURK. Where am I?

CONNIE. You are in St. Helena's Recovery Home. You were found naked and exhausted on the beach by the Matron. (*The* WOMAN *nods.*) She brought you back here and tended you with her own hands.

MATRON. You've been a most difficult patient. I had to give you injections to bring you up to par.

McTURK (*to* CONNIE). Don't send me back to prison. I couldn't bear it.

CONNIE. I've no intention of sending you back to prison. As long as you're sorry for what you did you'll be allowed to resume your normal life. What was your occupation?

McTURK. I have no occupation.

CONNIE. Then you'd better join the army. We're at war now, you know.

McTURK. War? How terrible. Who are we fighting?

CONNIE. The rebels, of course. Who else should we be fighting. You'll be with my regiment.

McTURK. But my sympathies lie entirely with your enemies.

CONNIE. I shall pretend I haven't heard that. (*To* MATRON.) See that he reaches the Recruitment Centre by 13.00 hours.

She marches away down the ward. The MATRON *bends over and kisses* McTURK.

MATRON. I'll be sorry to lose you, but you've a duty to do.

McTURK. Was anyone with me when I was found?

MATRON. No.

McTURK. I rescued a young woman from the sea. I wonder what became of her.

MATRON. She's dead, I expect. (*With a smile.*) I'll give you an alcohol rub before you go. As a sort of parting present.

She hurries away. McTURK *closes his eyes.*

107. Interior. A Recruitment Centre. *The hall is full of* WOMEN. *A few* MEN *are present. Recruiting posters line the walls. The main space of the room is taken up with booths in which the recruits fill up their forms. At the top of the room is a table on a platform. Sitting at the table are a number of high-ranking* ARMY OFFICERS. MRS O'SCULLION *sits with them. At the top of the table sits* CONNIE (*in uniform*). *She gets to her feet. Loud cheers.*

CONNIE (*smiling, waiting for silence*). As most of you know we are now at war. Our efforts to reach agreement with the rebels came to an abrupt end last night. Naturally there is dismay in official circles. Failure came after several hours of extra talks, optimism and the postponement of 'Pixie' Heath's trip abroad. A little note was left on my desk by 'Pixie' this morning. (*She picks up a note from in front of her.*) It reads, quite simply — (*She glances at the note.*) 'Men too much for me. Feel worn out. Personal charm a failure'. Acting on the advice of Dr Maud and the Rev Daisy Greene, I declared a state of war as existing from 13.00 hours.

Loud cheering. CONNIE *sits down. Uniformed* OFFICERS *pass round recruiting forms.* McTURK, *carrying his form, approaches one of the booths.* RAMSAY *takes the form from him.*

RAMSAY. I've already filled in your form.

McTURK. I wasn't going to fill it in. I was hoping to get rid of it.

CHRISTOPHER LOW *appears on the other side of* McTURK.

LOW. It's all been arranged. We've joined Field Marshal Boon's regiment.

RAMSAY. The tide of history is with women. You can't fight it. Their ideology is sounder.

Everyone stands to attention as CONNIE *leaves the platform. She stops beside* CHRISTOPHER LOW. *Smiles.*

CONNIE. Lovely to see you here. Are you joining the army?

LOW. Yes.

CONNIE. Good. It'll make a woman of you. (*Chucks him under the chin.*) Come and see me in my caravan. Talk over old times.

The uniformed WOMEN *allow her to pass. She sweeps from the Recruitment Centre to a burst of applause and* MARTIAL MUSIC.

108. Exterior. An Army Camp. *A little rain is falling. Tucked into a hollow the camp is floored with mud which the wheels of lorries have crossed with waterlogged furrows.* McTURK *meets* RAMSAY *on the edge of the muddy wasteland. They are both in uniform.* McTURK *shoulders a gun.*

McTURK. What happened to your patrol?

RAMSAY. It was wiped out in a skirmish two days ago.

McTURK. How did you escape?

RAMSAY. I ran away before the firing began.

McTURK. Did anybody see you?

RAMSAY. A master sergeant spotted me hiding behind an abandoned supply truck.

McTURK. What happened?

RAMSAY. I shot her. It was the first time I'd used a gun since the campaign began.

They trudge wearily towards a distant Troop Office.

109. Interior. The Troop Office. CONNIE *stands before a map.*
A blackboard with some battle positions marked stands to her
right. The hut is full of WOMEN OFFICERS *and* N.C.O.s. *A*
few MEN *are also present.* CHRISTOPHER LOW, *in a smart*
uniform, stands beside CONNIE. McTURK *and* RAMSAY
sit with the AUDIENCE.

CONNIE (*turning from the map with a bright smile*). We move
up tomorrow, dears.

> *A flutter of interest from the* WOMEN.

CONNIE. I'm sure we're all terribly excited by the prospect of a
real face to face meeting with a man! (*She chews on an*
unlighted cigarette.) The front is in a fluid state at the
moment so we've no definite news on how things will turn
out. The rendezvous will be at Reference 7.

> *She swings round and prods the map.*

CONNIE. Jean and Freddie have prepared haversack rations for
us. If any of you are on a diet please let Freddie know. He
won't be responsible for that 'extra poundage'. (*She laughs*
merrily.) Any questions?

McTURK. Are we winning?

CONNIE. Well, my dear, I'd rather not commit myself at the
moment. I had a long chatty letter from 'Pixie' yesterday.
And she's heard rumours — whilst having elevenses at
Tregunters — that the war will be over in time for the Spring
showings. So we mustn't lose heart.

> *She turns to* CHRISTOPHER LOW.

CONNIE. I want two signallers detailed tonight. And pick a
good-looking wireless operator for my set, will you?

> *She leaves the hut with a cheerful wave.*

110. Exterior. The battle area. Dawn. *In the distance guns are*
firing. Not heavy sustained fire, but sporadic bursts of one or
two rounds at a time. A jeep is driving rapidly along a road
blackened by shellbursts. CONNIE *is in front.* CHRISTOPHER
LOW *is driving. In the back sit* McTURK *and* JACK RAMSAY.
The jeep rounds a corner. The place is deserted. The jeep stops.
CONNIE *steps down.*

CONNIE. Dismount! We're going to establish camp over to the left. Bring the telephone. Quick now!

As they plunge into the scrub, the noise of firing increases. Bren guns chatter from a dozen different points. Sandwiched between comes the thud of INFANTRY MORTARS.

CONNIE. Heads down!

A shower of bullets falls across the path. Everyone ducks. They stumble across the open ground. WOMEN in uniform appear and salute CONNIE. A CONVOY drives up. Five hundred uniformed WOMEN jump down and begin to pitch camp.

111. Exterior. The new camp. Evening. *A little rain is falling. The camp resembles the old camp. McTURK, his head bandaged, his uniform muddy, meets RAMSAY who has his arm in a sling. Both are battle-stained and weary.*

RAMSAY. This camp is no different to the other one.

McTURK. It's nearer the enemy lines. The chances of being killed are greater. It's quite different.

RAMSAY. What happened to that little corporal you were keen on?

McTURK. She was drafted home on compassionate grounds.

RAMSAY. Why?

McTURK. Her husband has dyed his hair and gone on the streets.

RAMSAY. It always happens in wartime when the women are away.

They meet up with CHRISTOPHER LOW. His uniform is spotless.

LOW. The G.O.C. requests the pleasure of your company in the concert tent this evening. Our quota of entertainments has arrived. Now is the time to desert if you've been turning the matter over in your mind.

They turn a corner and meet a number of dancing MEN and WOMEN dressed in Brazilian costumes waving maraccas. Behind the carnival is a white-painted van. On the side of the

van is a painting of a South American scene with the words
'P. DRUMGOOLE. MUSIC IN THE SOUTHERN MANNER'.

*The van stops. MISS DRUMGOOLE steps out. She waves
with a gay smile.*

MISS DRUMGOOLE. It's cabaret time!

*The uniformed WOMEN begin dancing with the Brazilian
dance troupe. McTURK, RAMSAY and LOW rush to meet
MISS DRUMGOOLE. They embrace her. She lingers longest
in the arms of McTURK.*

MISS DRUMGOOLE. Oh, Ian McTurk, your kisses haven't
altered. You give a girl a most beautiful experience even
in public.

RAMSAY. What are you doing here?

MISS DRUMGOOLE. I'm a licensed entertainer. I travel round
the battlefields bringing hope and cheer to the weary soldier.

They link arms and take her towards a line of sagging tents.

LOW. We thought you were drowned.

MISS DRUMGOOLE. I was rescued by a passing ferry. When
war broke out I formed my Latin American dance band
from a group of discontented Welsh Nationalists. I've no
talent for South American rhythms, but I don't let this spoil
my enjoyment. But how did you escape the fury of the
elements?

RAMSAY. It would take too long to explain. Be thankful that
we're alive not to tell the story.

MISS DRUMGOOLE. Is there any special number you'd like
my band to play tonight. Bear in mind that we specialise in
songs with Latin American rhythms.

LOW. We'll have to miss your concert. We intend to desert.

MISS DRUMGOOLE. After my performance I have to cross
the enemy lines to sing to a man who is mortally wounded.
I have a visa. You'd better come with me.

They kiss her. She remains in IAN McTURK's arms.

MISS DRUMGOOLE. Oh, Ian McTurk, you're the nicest man
I've ever met. Won't you please marry me when the war is over?

McTURK. No. My heart is broken. Don't ever ask me again.

He turns and walks away. MISS DRUMGOOLE *watches sadly.*

112. Exterior. Night. A road across the battlefields. *Barbed wire. Dug-outs. The sound of shells bursting. Flashes on the horizon.* MISS DRUMGOOLE's *van stops at a checkpoint. A* SENTRY *comes forward holding a rifle. He is revealed, in the dim light, as the* LORD MAYOR (TERENCE O'SCULLION). MISS DRUMGOOLE *hands him some documents.* McTURK *puts his head out of the car.*

McTURK. Aren't you Terence O'Scullion, the one-time Lord Mayor?

The MAYOR *stares hard. Smiles.*

MAYOR. Yes. And you're Ian McTurk. What are you doing here?

McTURK. We're going to join up with the rebels.

MAYOR. How I wish that I could do the same. I don't like working for my sergeant. She's a most unpleasant woman.

MISS DRUMGOOLE. There's room in the back. Why don't you join us?

MAYOR. How kind you are. I don't deserve your friendship after the unkind way I behaved on Bernie's yacht before the war.

They open the door. He gets in.

113. Interior. The van. MISS DRUMGOOLE *is driving. The* MAYOR *sits with the others in the back.*

McTURK. Why are you dressed as a private soldier?

MAYOR. I am a private soldier. When we landed from Bernie's yachting expedition I was arrested on suspicion of having aided the rebels during the riots after the death of the late Prime Minister. Although I was acquitted at my trial, my property was confiscated. I've been penniless ever since.

RAMSAY. What happened to Bernard Coates?

MAYOR. He left Rowena and took to playing the piano professionally.

McTURK. How is Rowena?

MAYOR. She's still the most modern woman in the world. I saw her only yesterday selling war-bonds. She's very much against the establishment.

RAMSAY'S FATHER *is seen on the road waving the car to a halt. MISS DRUMGOOLE applies the brakes.*

RAMSAY'S FATHER. Oh, thank God! I'm wounded! Please get me to the nearest hospital.

McTURK. Get in the back. We're going over to the rebels.

114. Interior. The back of the van. RAMSAY'S FATHER *is white-faced and shaken. Blood pours down his ragged tunic.*

McTURK. Aren't you Jack Ramsay's father?

RAMSAY'S FATHER. I was before the war. I don't know who I am now.

RAMSAY. What are you doing wounded by the side of an arterial road? I thought you were leading our boys to victory.

RAMSAY'S FATHER. I made a dreadful mess of leading our boys to victory. They were going to put me before a firing squad only they couldn't afford the bullets. So I was marched into a wood to be hung like a common criminal. As we entered the forest, we were caught in enemy cross-fire and I escaped. I'm going over to the rebels. They know how to make a man feel he's wanted.

McTURK. We'll have you safe and sound in a well-run all-male hospital in next to no time.

RAMSAY'S FATHER *looks horrified.*

RAMSAY'S FATHER. What are you talking about? I'm going to join the rebels.

McTURK. The men.

RAMSAY'S FATHER. No. The women. I can't go back to the men; they've sworn to court martial me. Oh, what a fool I was to get mixed up with you! (*He seizes the wheel of the van.*) Back! Back to the women! Our only hope!

MISS DRUMGOOLE. No! The men! We must go on!

They struggle with the wheel. The van swerves wildly. The
MAYOR *leans forward and speaks to* MISS DRUMGOOLE.

MAYOR. This road is heavily mined. Pull into the side road and
let's discuss the matter sensibly.

MISS DRUMGOOLE *swings the van into a side road. A loud
explosion shakes the van. In a blinding flash of light a sign is
seen* 'LANDMINES — DANGER!' *Another explosion wrecks
the van.* McTURK *is flung out onto the road. The van is
blown to pieces in succeeding explosions. Blackness.*

115. Interior. A hospital ward. McTURK *is in bed. He is wrapped
from head to foot in bandages. A blood transfusion unit is
beside him. He stares vacantly at the ceiling. A bell rings. Visitors
enter. They go to the other beds.* RAMSAY *and* CHRISTOPHER
LOW *enter. They sit next to* McTURK. LOW *unwraps a bunch
of grapes he has brought and begins to eat them.*

RAMSAY. We've joined the rebels. We couldn't wait for you
to recover. You've been unconscious for weeks.

LOW. Bernard Coates is our commanding officer. Rowena broke
his heart.

RAMSAY. My father was left to die by the side of the road.
The fortunes of war. We were rescued by a rebel ambulance
and he was a declared Government supporter. Miss Drumgoole's
hair fell out. She's taken to wearing a wig.

LOW. Yesterday a species of louse caused a whole battalion to
report sick. The M.O. had them sprayed with a new kind of
drug which killed ten men and brought the others out in a
kind of virulent rash.

RAMSAY. The rest of us are enduring the lice.

LOW *scratches himself. A* DOCTOR *hurries up. He picks up
a hypodermic syringe and gives* McTURK *an injection.
A bell rings.* McTURK *closes his eyes.*

LOW. You're much better. You're to be allowed to join us
tomorrow.

116. Exterior. The rebel encampment. MEN *in uniform pass to
and fro across the muddy waste. An ambulance drives into the*

centre of the camp. The door is opened and McTURK *gets down.* RAMSAY *meets him.*

RAMSAY. I'm glad you're well again. We're rather short of rations at the moment. Did you bring any grapes from the hospital?

McTURK. No.

LOW, *in a smart uniform, ambles up.*

LOW. What are we fighting for? We've been having an argument back there.

RAMSAY. Consult the handbook. You'll find a list of things we're fighting for at the back with the map of the London Underground.

BERNARD COATES *hurries up, pulling on his gloves.*

BERNARD COATES. The enemy forces are only a mile away. I've ordered a retreat. Commandeer every vehicle and drive for your lives!

They leap into the ambulance. MEN *are running in all directions. A lorry rumbles into the camp.* McTURK *starts up the ambulance which shoots forward and crashes into the oncoming lorry. The lorry and the ambulance burst into flames and are wrecked. A number of* MEN *run up with stretchers. They take* McTURK, RAMSAY, LOW *and* BERNARD COATES, *pale with shock, from the ambulance and put them on stretchers. They do the same for the driver of the lorry.*

Two ambulances drive into the camp, their bells ringing. Male NURSES *and* DOCTORS *leap from each ambulance. They pick up the stretchers and put them into the ambulances. The two ambulances drive off. They are hardly out of the camp when they run over a landmine which explodes under them. The two ambulances burst into flames. Injured and horrified* MEN *stumble out.*

MEN *run up with stretchers. They take the injured crews and passengers of both ambulances from the shadow of the burning wreckage. They wrap them all in blankets. Four ambulances drive into the camp.* DOCTORS *and* MALE NURSES *leap from them. The* VICTIMS *of the explosion and the motor accident are piled into the four ambulances. They drive off. A retreat is sounded on a trumpet.*

Lorries rumble into retreat positions and drive with the four ambulances away from the camp. Outside the camp is a hump-backed bridge fording a stream. As the lorries and ambulances drive over it the bridge collapses. Lorries and ambulances crash into the stream amid the wreckage from the bridge. Explosions. Flames. Panic.

MEN with stretchers rescue the, by now, shocked, injured and well-nigh senseless, McTURK, RAMSAY and LOW. They are placed, wrapped in blankets, with other VICTIMS of the various disasters. The banks of the stream and the approaches to the camp are lined with the dead and injured. In the stream are four wrecked and blazing ambulances. Outside the camp are two wrecked and blazing ambulances. Inside the camp is a wrecked and blazing ambulance and a wrecked and blazing lorry.

With bells ringing furiously eight ambulances drive into the disaster area. NURSES and DOCTORS leap from the ambulances and pile McTURK, RAMSAY and LOW and the other VICTIMS into them. The eight ambulances drive off.

At this point the camp is surrounded and attacked by Government troops led by CONNIE and RAMSAY'S FATHER. Hand grenades are thrown and the ambulances set on fire. Hundreds of MEN with stretchers attempt to put the injured, the dying, the sick, unhappy army of VICTIMS into some sort of shape. To the injured of the many disasters are added the MEN wounded by the attacking troops. A whole fleet of ambulances arrive with their bells ringing.

At this point, with snipers' fire, the defence of the camp, blazing ambulances, the cries of pain, the panic created by the appearance of the enemy, the stretcher bearers are hard put to it to know where to turn. Stretcher bearers pick up McTURK. Shots are fired and the stretcher bearers collapse as badly injured as their patient. More stretcher bearers pick up the stretcher bearers. They are hit in their turn and collapse. The victims and the helpers struggle together in the mud of the battlefield.

An army of ambulances moves away from the camp. McTURK, RAMSAY and LOW run after them. At this point, with a loud roar, the earth caves in and the ambulances, full of suffering humanity, crash into the hole which has opened up in the treacherous subsoil.

An army of stretcher bearers attempts to bring order to the scene. Several descend upon McTURK, RAMSAY and LOW. Seeing what has happened before, they decline to be helped and fight off the stretcher bearers. The stretcher bearers, injured now from the blows inflicted by the YOUNG MEN, are swept away to the First Aid Sections by other stretcher bearers.

All this with the sound of rifle and Bren gun fire. Bells ringing. Trumpets sounding retreat. Shouts and screams from the injured. Blood pouring from bleeding wounds. On the edge of a gaping hole amid the carnage of battle. Onto the scene steps FATHER BRODIE, holding high the CROSS upon which OUR LORD died, accompanied by NUNS and CHOIR BOYS singing a Hymn to the Glory of Immortal God.

CHRISTOPHER LOW, struck dumb, kneels. McTURK bursts into tears and sits sobbing among the stretchers and the blankets. RAMSAY shrieks with maniacal laughter and begins to leap about in a kind of glee.

The three YOUNG MEN are surrounded by WOMEN armed with rifles and led away.

117. Interior. The Government H.Q. *CONNIE and a number of WOMEN officers. RAMSAY'S FATHER is with them. McTURK, RAMSAY and LOW are led in. CONNIE turns to them.*

McTURK. I suppose you're going to have us shot as traitors?

CONNIE. Traitors? (*She looks surprised.*) Of course not.

RAMSAY'S FATHER. You've just won the Military Cross.

RAMSAY. Why?

CONNIE. For exceptional bravery over and above the call of duty.

RAMSAY'S FATHER. Your strategy in ramming that approaching lorry resulted in a chain reaction which completely immobilised the enemy.

CONNIE. The war is over! You're all heroes!

CONNIE, RAMSAY'S FATHER and the OFFICERS all embrace the YOUNG MEN with great emotion.

CONNIE (*to* LOW). It only remains to announce the date of our wedding.

RAMSAY'S FATHER (*to* RAMSAY). Your mother was shot by a sniper last week. She's to receive the O.B.E. posthumously. My joy is complete.

McTURK. But the peace brings no joy to me. I can never marry the woman I love.

He turns and leaves the room.

118. Exterior. The battlefield, *recently the scene of such horror, is now transformed. Dancing figures reel among the debris, the lorries and ambulances still blazing provide light for courting couples. Among them are one or two bandaged figures. Bloody bandages flutter like ribbons in a light breeze.*

119. Exterior. The Town Hall square. *The victory celebrations. Many people are decorating war heroes.* MRS O'SCULLION *allows the injured to kiss her hand.* FATHER BRODIE *gives them his blessing. Dancing and cheering.*

120. Interior. Money-Box Lodge. *Chandeliers and dancing to a waltz. Crowds of people.* CONNIE, ROWENA, BERNARD COATES *and* RAMSAY'S FATHER (*in a magnificent Field-Marshal's uniform heavy with medals*) *stand with* RAMSAY *under an enormous oil painting of a pair of feet.*

CONNIE (*to* RAMSAY). And what are you going to get up to now that the war is over?

RAMSAY. I'm going to tell the patrons of the Ritz that the manager is mad.

CONNIE (*turns to* ROWENA *and* BERNARD COATES *with a laugh*). Isn't that absolutely splendid? He's going to tell people that the manager of the Ritz is mad. He's such a convincing liar too.

RAMSAY'S FATHER. It isn't a lie. The manager of the Ritz is mad.

BERNARD COATES (*with a cough*). Any well-regulated society must find room for anti-social activity. (*He smiles in a kindly way to* RAMSAY.) I hope you have a great success in your enterprise.

ROWENA *opens her eyes wide and looks intelligent.*

ROWENA. I'm inclined to believe that perhaps the manager of the Ritz is mad.

CONNIE. You're so bitter against the establishment, aren't you dear?

BERNARD COATES (*to* RAMSAY). My wife, as I expect you know, has been elected the most modern woman in the world for another year.

McTURK, *rather drunk, appears at* ROWENA's *side. He puts an arm round her waist.*

McTURK. Will you marry me?

ROWENA *gives a squeaky laugh and pushes his arm away.*

ROWENA (*smiling to* CONNIE *and* BERNARD COATES). Isn't he terrible? But I think startling people ought to be encouraged.

McTURK. Come for a walk in the garden.

He leads her away.

121. Exterior. A garden. Moonlight. *Dark leaves. Roses. A nightingale. Faintly blown by the wind comes the sound of a waltz.* McTURK *walks with* ROWENA *under a rose arbour.*

McTURK. I love you, Rowena. Through all my sufferings you've been constantly in my thoughts.

ROWENA *smiles an uncomfortable smile.*

ROWENA. Shall we go in? It's turning cold.

McTURK. I've kept this rose you gave me. (*He takes it from his pocket.*) It's been watered with my tears. It was for your sake I did everything. Why did you have to break my heart? I loved you so much.

ROWENA *turns to go. He takes her hand.*

ROWENA. I must go! Love seems out of place in a garden in the moonlight.

McTURK. I'd hoped that some day we might settle down. Even get married.

ROWENA. That's not possible. I've a rich husband whom I love dearly.

McTURK. Then we must part forever. I can't go on seeing you. There's an ache in my heart that can never be eased or satisfied.

She draws near him.

McTURK. Kiss me before we say goodbye.

Petals from a rose fall softly upon them from an overhanging bough. The moonlight folds them in a shining embrace as they kiss before parting forever.

122. Interior. Money-Box Lodge. CHRISTOPHER LOW *is talking to the* MAYOR (TERENCE O'SCULLION).

LOW. What happened to you after the landmine exploded.

MAYOR. I was in the most desperate straits for nearly a year. Then I had a stroke of luck and profited by it. I spent the last six months of the war directing operations from a wheelchair.

LOW. But you were only a private.

MAYOR. I was mistaken for a General who'd been admitted to hospital for a minor surgical operation. I should've owned up, I suppose. But there it is. We're all human and err sometimes.

LOW. How did you get to be Lord Mayor again?

MAYOR. That was due entirely to the influence of the General I was impersonating. He'd been rather badly treated as a private soldier and he paid me a large sum of money to regain his identity. With his cheque in my pocket I was soon up to my old tricks on the stock exchange. I'm now twice as wealthy as I was.

He accepts a glass of champagne from a passing waiter.

MAYOR. But what's been happening to you? You're quite a hero, I'm told.

LOW. Yes. I've been decorated for bravery in the field and now I'm going to marry my commanding officer.

MAYOR. What a unique experience! You'll be able to sell your story to the newspapers.

LOW. I shan't, I'm afraid. You see, my wife will be the President. (*He shows the* MAYOR *his engagement ring.*) My private life will be top secret from now on. I shall probably be offered a post in the cabinet.

The MAYOR *looks surprised.*

MAYOR. But only women qualify for Government office. A new law has just been passed.

LOW. You must be mistaken. Connie would never consent to such inhuman legislation.

He turns to RAMSAY'S FATHER *who happens to be passing.*

LOW. Where's the President?

RAMSAY'S FATHER. She's waiting for you under the little picture of Jesus in the conservatory.

123. Interior. The conservatory. CHRISTOPHER LOW *enters pushing aside the leaves.* CONNIE *stands under a palm tree. She gives him a brief, welcoming smile. Takes out a cigar case.*

CONNIE. Cigar?

LOW. You know I never smoke.

CONNIE. It's a chocolate one. Your favourite brand.

   LOW *takes a cigar from the case. He unwraps the band and eats the cigar.* CONNIE *lights a real cigar. They sit together on a rustic seat.*

LOW (*petulantly*). What's this ridiculous new law? The days have gone when I could pass as a woman. I have to shave twice a week now.

CONNIE. Men shouldn't concern themselves with making laws. (*Stroking his hair.*) They should be charming and masculine. Give mummy a kiss and forget about it.

   He pushes her away.

LOW. What about the equality of the sexes? Isn't that what Mrs Pankhurst wanted?

CONNIE. I'm sure she didn't, dear. Women have never imagined that they were equal to men. They've always known that they were superior.

LOW *is quite put out by her reply.*

CONNIE. This law is only the first. I hope ultimately to exclude men from Parliament, the armed services, the law, medicine and the Church.

LOW *stands. Tight-lipped.*

LOW. I can't possibly marry a woman who holds those views. (*He pulls off his engagement ring.*) Take back your ring! I never want to see you again.

He flings the ring at her feet and leaves the conservatory.

124. Exterior. The garden. RAMSAY, McTURK *and* LOW *wander through the dew-laden foliage under a lightening sky.*

LOW. I'm going to sell the trinkets Connie gave me. I always hated her loud and vulgar presents.

McTURK. What kind of presents were they?

LOW. Diamond cuff-links and the occasional gold cigarette-case.

McTURK. I shall send Rowena a dozen red roses each year on the anniversary of our parting. The card will say simply — 'McTurk — Rowena — Always'. I can't bear to think of the long years of loneliness that lie ahead.

RAMSAY. My father is going to marry the matron of St. Helena's Recovery Home. He hasn't benefited from his past mistakes.

125. Exterior. A deserted street. The sun rising. *The young men wander past closed shops, under an arcade to a memorial commemorating some long forgotten war. Under a badly damaged allegorical statue of 'Peace' stands* MISS DRUMGOOLE *bathed in early sunlight. She wears spectacles. She has on a plain hat and coat. She is carrying a small case. Her face is stained with tears.*
The YOUNG MEN *run to her. They embrace her.*

McTURK. I thought you'd been killed in the war.

MISS DRUMGOOLE. No. I survived. I was very ill for a time, but I'm glad to say that I'm quite recovered. I can't see as well as I did. And my hair never regained its original lustre. I survived, though, if not in one piece at least in recognisable shapes.

LOW. Where are you going?

MISS DRUMGOOLE. To the railway station. I've accepted a post as children's nurse with a large family in New Guinea. It's rather a hazardous undertaking.

RAMSAY. Why? Do they eat their old nurses?

MISS DRUMGOOLE. In certain circumstances I believe they do.

McTURK *suddenly flings his arms about her.*

McTURK. Who wants to be a Governess in a cannibal kraal? Leave these head-hunters to their own devices and marry me.

MISS DRUMGOOLE *is bowled over by his generous offer.*

MISS DRUMGOOLE. But you love Miss Rowena.

McTURK. My heart is broken, but everything else is in working order. I'd make an excellent husband.

MISS DRUMGOOLE. What would we live on?

LOW. If you married me I'd sell my jewels.

McTURK. The Mayor would be delighted to show us how to make money from dishonest dealings on the Stock Exchange.

MISS DRUMGOOLE. I can't marry both of you.

RAMSAY. Why not? The President has just introduced new legislation to permit a woman to have three husbands. Let's spend the rest of our lives as a quartette.

MISS DRUMGOOLE. No. You'd desert me to raise a rebellion.

RAMSAY. I wouldn't. Getting married and having children is the most rebellious thing a man can do. It shows a disregard for the conventional bourgeois status-quo and a fine, careless anarchic sense of the absurd.

MISS DRUMGOOLE. Very well. As long as its perfectly legal I will marry you.

They hug and kiss her on all parts of her body simultaneously. She gasps for breath and closes her eyes in ecstasy.

126. Interior A church. A fashionable congregation. FATHER
BRODIE *stands at the altar with a prayer book open. A rustle of
anticipation as the organ begins 'Here comes the bride'. The
congregation rises.* RAMSAY, McTURK *and* LOW *are at the
altar. With them is the* MAYOR (TERENCE O'SCULLION) *as
best man.* MISS DRUMGOOLE *is led down the aisle by*
BERNARD COATES. *Bridesmaids and* MRS O'SCULLION *as*
MATRON OF HONOUR. *The* BRIDE *reaches the altar. Gives*
RAMSAY, McTURK *and* LOW *a smile.* FATHER BRODIE
begins the service.

FATHER BRODIE. Dearly beloved, we are gathered here in
the sight of God, and in the face of this congregation to join
together these men and this woman in Holy Matrimony . . .

FATHER BRODIE's *voice becomes fainter. The candles
gutter at the altar. The ceremony wears on.* FATHER BRODIE
turns a page in the prayer book. He faces the boys.

FATHER BRODIE. Ian, John, Christopher wilt thou have this
woman to thy wedded wife?

THE BOYS. We will.

FATHER BRODIE. Patricia wilt thou have these men to thy
wedded husbands?

MISS DRUMGOOLE. I will.

127. Interior. The church. RAMSAY, McTURK *and* LOW *lead*
MISS DRUMGOOLE *down the aisle to the accompaniment of
the wedding march.*

128. Exterior. The church steps. *Confetti is thrown. Bridesmaids.
Friends. Well-wishers. A photographer runs forward.*

PHOTOGRAPHER (*pushing people aside*). Just the happy
quartette, if you don't mind!

He kneels. MISS DRUMGOOLE *and the young men pose for
their wedding photograph. A flash.*

129. Interior. A hotel corridor. RAMSAY'S FATHER, *in the
uniform of a hotel page, leads* MISS DRUMGOOLE *and the
young men up to a door.*

McTURK (*to* RAMSAY'S FATHER). The last time I saw you was at the Victory celebrations. You were wearing a Field Marshal's uniform.

RAMSAY'S FATHER (*wheezing, opening the door*). I was a Field Marshal then, now I'm a hotel page. Only the uniform is the same. I'm married to the ex-Matron of the Recovery Home who treats me with the contempt I deserve. My home life makes sorry telling. You'll find no comfort in marriage. Everything's in a state of flux. (*He shakes his head, coughs a little.*) We live in an era of constant change and extreme conservatism. I'm on duty at six tomorrow. Ring when you require breakfast.

He stumbles away down the corridor. The young men lift their wife up and carry her across the threshold.

130. Interior. The hotel bedroom. Morning. *The sun streams into the room.* MISS DRUMGOOLE *is in bed with* RAMSAY, McTURK *and* LOW.

MISS DRUMGOOLE. It's like a wonderful dream! I hope we have a long and happy married life!

The young men kiss her. There is a struggle. MISS DRUMGOOLE *squeals with delight and disappears under the coverlet with her husbands.*

The end.